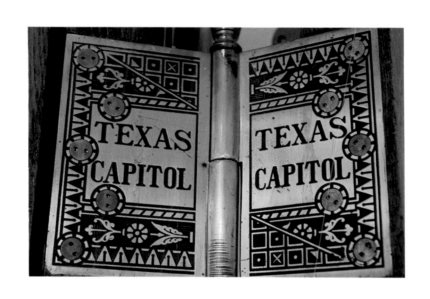

THE CAPITOL OF TEXAS

A LEGEND IS REBORN

This pictorial tour of the Lone Star statehouse, presented by staff members of the Austin American-Statesman, is dedicated to all Texans, past, present and future.

LONGSTREET PRESS, INC.
Atlanta, Georgia

Special thanks to the State Preservation Board and its staff, especially Executive Director Dealey Decherd Herndon, for their help in making this book possible

Photography by Larry Kolvoord, Ralph Barrera, Sung Park, Lynne Dobson, Taylor Johnson, David Kennedy, Tom Lankes and Ted S. Warren

Text by Michael E. Ward

Graphics by Robert Dorrell

Historical photos courtesy of the Texas State Library, State Preservation Board, Austin History Center, Texas Senate and Texas House of Representatives

Edited by Maggie Balough, Laylan Copelin, Ruth B. Ward and Diane Porter

Photographic editing by Jay Godwin and Zach Ryall

Research editing by Cyndi Hughes and Denise Haney

Art direction by Gretchen Heber

Page i: *One of the Capitol's brass hinges.* **Page ii:** *Craggy lines of the Capitol's exterior were to have been more refined, but a change to granite as the exterior stone simplified the building's lines.* **Page iii:** *Mirroring the star atop the Capitol's inside dome is this one at the center of the Capitol Extension's Central Court.* **Facing page:** *Colorful Fourth of July blast in 1993 provides a spectacular backdrop for the lighted Capitol dome.*

Printed in the United States of America

1st Printing, 1995

Library of Congress Catalog Number: 94-74242

ISBN: 1-56352-196-2

Published in 1995 by Longstreet Press, Inc., a subsidiary of Cox Newspapers, a division of Cox Enterprises, Inc.
2140 Newmarket Parkway, Suite 118, Marietta, Georgia 30067

Printed by Horowitz/Rae, Cedar Grove, New Jersey

Electronic film prep and separations by Advertising Technologies Inc., Atlanta, GA

CONTENTS

FOREWORD

George W. Bush
Forty-sixth Governor of Texas

The original construction of our Texas Capitol in the late 1800s and its magnificent restoration more than a century later prove that what Texans can dream, Texans can do.

The magnificent pink granite building is more than the nerve center of state government. It is a living museum of Texas history. The most recent restoration was the most extensive in the Capitol's history; the need to repair the building, however, was almost as old as the Capitol itself.

When construction workers completed the building in 1888, more than 20,000 proud Texans poured into Austin from around the state to marvel at its design and to participate in the dedication ceremony. Unfortunately, the crowd almost rioted when the Capitol roof leaked during a heavy thunderstorm.

The Capitol's roof was repaired soon after, but the challenge of maintaining and preserving the home of Texas' government continued to confront state leaders. As Texas grew, the Capitol's office space became cramped, original furniture was damaged, and much of the building's architectural uniqueness was obscured behind temporary walls and layers of plaster.

In 1990 the State Preservation Board undertook the daunting task of restoring and expanding the Capitol. Five years later, when members of the Seventy-Fourth Legislature arrived at their offices, many of them thought they had stepped into a time machine that had transported them back 100 years. The grandeur of the past had been restored, yet the convenience of a modern office building maintained. The oak, pine and cherry wainscoting had been painstakingly reconstructed; century-old brass hinges engraved with the words "Texas Capitol" once again held the heavy wood doors in position, and Capitol furniture, once discarded or sold, had been retrieved, restored and returned to the legislators' offices.

THE CAPITOL OF TEXAS

Nowhere is the State Preservation Board's hard work more evident than in the Governor's original office. Until the early 1930s, the Governor's office was located on the first floor of the Capitol and was one of the few rooms in the building with carpeting, draperies and mahogany furniture. The State Preservation Board used historical photographs, inventories and furnishing specifications that survived over the years to recreate the room. Even the Governor's historic curtain desk, believed to have been sold decades ago, was located after an extensive search.

The more than one million people a year who visit the Capitol may now step back into Texas history. Floor mosaics commemorate the twelve great battles in Texas' past, and glass cases display the six flags that have flown over our state. Thanks to the State Preservation Board's ability to dream big dreams, our Capitol will be enjoyed by today's Texans and preserved for future generations.

Laura and I want to thank everyone associated with the Capitol restoration project. Texas has always succeeded because our citizens are not afraid of challenges and are blessed with the ingenuity and perseverance to find creative solutions. Our majestic Capitol stands as a living monument to that can-do spirit.

***Facing page:** The silhouette of a bronze statue of a volunteer firefighter, carrying a frightened child in one arm and a lantern in his other hand, stands in silent tribute at the Capitol's south entry. The monument was erected in 1896 to honor Texas volunteers who have lost their lives fighting fires.*

*I*n May 1888, when Texas opened its pink-granite statehouse crowning an Austin hilltop, the Capitol defined not so much what the state was as what it was to become.

At that time, the Lone Star State did not need the seventh-largest building in the world to house its cash-strapped government. But Texans, eyeing their destiny, wanted it.

Their leaders found a way: They traded 3,050,000 acres of public land in the Panhandle, vast prairies that crossed ten counties, for a Victorian-era showplace with a dome that, fittingly, is taller than that of the nation's Capitol.

The Capitol is a place where rough-cut cowboys, oil barons and high-tech entrepreneurs have met on common ground, where the rich and the poor have staked their claims as equal owners.

Through the years, since the Capitol doors opened, Texas has grown as a state. It has truly become worthy of such a Capitol. Yet the monu-

Destiny in Granite

ment was almost lost. A 1983 fire spurred a restoration unlike any other. Texans buried an addition to the Capitol, then restored the treasured statehouse to its century-old grandeur. The legend was enlarged, the original vision preserved.

No other state has a Capitol like it. But no other state is like Texas.

Above: Horse-drawn buggies carried traffic on the Capitol's southeast drive after the turn of the century. ***Facing page:*** Afternoon sunlight highlights the rounded lines of the Capitol's dome. The building's designer originally proposed a square tower instead.

THE CAPITOL OF TEXAS

Above: Renaissance Revival style of the Capitol, based on the architecture of 15th-century Italy, is evident in the dome's rounded arches and classical design features. *Right:* The most recognizable feature of the statehouse shines in a summer sunset. Though the dome matches the granite building in color and distant appearance, it is mostly made of metal, not stone. *Facing page:* Like a pair of bright eyes, room lights in the dark Capitol illuminate a solitary painter touching up restoration work in 1994.

The triumphal entry arch of the Capitol's south facade presents an imposing image in Burnet County granite. The Capitol's builder called the stone red granite, although it is now commonly referred to as pink granite.

THE CAPITOL OF TEXAS

*Fading daylight slowly transforms
the lantern atop the dome into a
nighttime beacon beneath the
Goddess of Liberty statue. The star
is gilded with 23 carat gold leaf.
The statue is a replica, put in place
in June 1986 following a tour of six
Texas cities. Removed because of
corrosion by the elements, the
original is now in a museum.*

Right: Bolts of lightning skitter across the nighttime sky, illuminating the Capitol dome with an eerie glow. **Pages 10 and 11:** *From its site atop what once was called Capitol Square, the statehouse is now surrounded by the city. The view looking north shows state office buildings and the University of Texas beyond.*

THE CAPITOL OF TEXAS

Dawn was still an hour away when Mark White, roused from his slumber inside the Governor's Mansion, sensed something wrong. Sirens wailed, more than the usual cacophony of Austin at night.

The sounds seemed to be stopping nearby.

When he phoned the Mansion security office, the voice at the other end confirmed the worst: "Some sort of a fire over there at the Capitol."

White dressed hurriedly and darted into the chilly air. He saw what Texas governors for years had feared would happen on their watch: From the east wing of the domed statehouse trailed a plume of dense, gray smoke, tinted an eerie crimson by the flashing emergency lights of fire trucks.

The Capitol was burning.

It was February 6, 1983 — a day in which history seemed poised to repeat itself. Fire had enveloped two previous Capitols in Austin, in 1881 and 1899.

All White could do was watch from the Capi-

Rebirth from Ashes

tol lawn, huddled with other worried state officials. The wait was frustrating and emotional. Some people wept.

After all, the burning structure was more than just a building. It was the Texas Capitol, the seat of state government, a revered and aged symbol of Lone Star greatness, a place where generations of schoolchildren — including White — had learned real-life history lessons while on field trips.

White, who had been governor for three weeks, prayed for a miracle.

Above: A smoldering shell is all that remains of the 1852 Capitol, destroyed in 1881 by a fire blamed on an improperly installed stove. One hundred and two years later, a smoky fire nearly destroyed the statehouse that replaced it. **Facing page:** *The dome looms high as firefighters work to extinguish the 1983 blaze.*

Wisps of smoke above the Capitol's East Wing spelled near-tragedy in the 1983 fire, which gutted the lieutenant governor's apartment. A faulty television set was blamed.

As White talks about that February morning now, years later, one can hear the emotion in his voice: "That's the most spectacular building in the state and the most historic building. With the exception of the Alamo, it's the one building that means more to all Texans than any other. And we came very close to losing it."

Within minutes, in fact. So pessimistic were firefighters at one point that they told White and other state officials to retrieve valuable papers before the fire spread to their offices.

For what seemed an eternity, the flames climbed elusively inside the plaster walls and through a maze of false ceilings, the result of years of makeshift remodelings. But thanks to modern equipment and some old-fashioned luck, firefighters were able to stop the fiery advance before the attic was engulfed.

The building was saved.

Watching the flames that February night, White and other officials acknowledged what had to be done. The Capitol had to be made safe for posterity.

What a fitting way for Texas to celebrate its 150th birthday in 1986, White thought.

Then history intervened again. Just as Texas was strapped for cash when it built the 1888 statehouse, so were its fortunes limited a century later.

The state's boom times had gone bust, and the budget was drenched in red ink. Taxpayer money for a complete overhaul was out of the question, and private fund-raising could not collect enough for all the work that needed to be done.

White did not have the choice that Texas pioneers had a century earlier; a chunk of the Texas Panhandle prairie could not be traded to pay for it.

White would reason years later: "When you're out of money, it's a little hard to be spending a whole heck of a lot of it on the Capitol... It was just not something I wanted to go raise taxes for, frankly."

White did what he could, mostly with private donations: The legislative chambers, several rooms and the Goddess of Liberty statue atop the dome were refurbished. But a total restoration remained on hold.

Things changed in 1987.

William P. Clements Jr. was back in the governor's office. Defeated for reelection four years earlier by White, a Democrat, the Dallas Republican had returned the favor to his political nemesis.

With him came a personal goal to restore the Capitol. And, at the same time, show up his rival.

The restoration was a topic on which White and Clements could agree — perhaps the only one, as White later would say.

Clements was a millionaire businessman — conservative, tough-edged, a no-new-taxes kind of fellow with a sometimes pugnacious demeanor. To him, the Capitol restoration was unfinished business, a personal priority for a second term he had thought would begin four years earlier.

As flames burned inside the Capitol in 1983, Gov. Mark White, left, Jerry Chapman of the lieutenant governor's office, center, and Lt. Gov. Bill Hobby watch from the lawn.

THE CAPITOL OF TEXAS

A gutted hallway behind the Senate Chamber stands as grim testament to the near-tragedy in 1983. Firefighters survey the damage just hours after the fire had been extinguished. From the ashes began a twelve-year effort that resulted in the complete restoration of the statehouse.

Reflections

In 1934, when Claudia Alta Taylor traveled to Washington, a girlfriend slipped her the name, address and phone number of someone the friend thought she should meet.

Lyndon Baines Johnson was then an administrative aide to Texas Congressman Dick Kleberg. The friend advised: "You'll just love him ... He'll show you around." Claudia Taylor, Lady Bird to her family, did not call. "I never intended to," she said.

That fall, though, she met him anyway, through a chance encounter in the Capitol. It forever changed their lives.

Miss Taylor, then 21, attending the University of Texas, had gone to the statehouse to see a friend who was working for the Texas Railroad Commission. Inside the office sat Johnson, thin but good-looking, with lots of black wavy hair. "An impressive young man," she recalls.

He invited her and their mutual friend to go out after work. And she met him for breakfast the next morning at the Driskill Hotel, their first date.

Johnson immediately was smitten with her, and she with him. By mid-November, they were married.

Lady Bird Johnson addresses legislators in the House Chamber in March 1989.

The friend who introduced Lady Bird Johnson to Lyndon in the Capitol also introduced her to the statehouse itself.

In April 1930, while she was attending an Episcopal girls' school in Dallas, Mrs. Johnson toured the huge granite edifice for the first time.

In school, she had studied photographs of the great buildings of Europe. The Texas Capitol, she remembers thinking, was on a par with the grandeur of those European buildings. Mrs. Johnson marveled at how grand, how "quite magnificent," the storied statehouse was.

During that first visit, she recalls examining every painting of the governors that were displayed in the Rotunda.

For Mrs. Johnson, a country girl from the small East Texas town of Karnack, the Capitol's ornate brass hardware and etched-glass appointments were fine, "like jewelry," she remembers thinking. Even during her many years in Washington, while Johnson served as congressman, senator, vice president and finally as president, she never forgot that magnificence.

Today, that first impression of the Texas statehouse remains little changed.

The Capitol is "a very elegant, sophisticated and handsome building," says the former First Lady. "I thought so then ... still do." ★

Clements was uniquely qualified. A longtime student of Texas history, he had purchased an abandoned brick school building in downtown Dallas a decade earlier and had restored it for his company headquarters.

During his first term, he and his wife, Rita, had raised private donations to restore the Governor's Mansion, an 1856 Greek Revival residence that had fallen into disrepair.

Clements had toured almost every statehouse in the nation, and knew how special the Texas Capitol is. "There isn't any other state Capitol that even comes close to comparing to our Capitol — in architectural design, in just plain old mass, m-a-s-s," he said.

The first hurdle for Clements — and Lt. Gov. Bill Hobby and House Speaker Gib Lewis, who supported the plan — was to persuade legislators to move from the Capitol. The building was too crowded and some would have to move elsewhere if it was to be properly restored. Clements also needed a master plan, a blueprint for the restoration.

Enter Allen McCree, an architect for the University of Texas System who was hired in September, 1988. His marching orders: Move the project forward. Quickly.

McCree, who knew the Capitol's flaws as well as its history, relished the challenge.

A native of Graham, a small town in northern Texas, McCree had spent hours at the Capitol while he was an architecture student at the University of Texas; he had sketched the cascading cast-iron staircases for class projects. Years later, in the 1970s, he studied the building in preparation for giving an after-dinner program for legislators. He became convinced that the venerable seat of government was endangered by its deteriorated condition; for several years thereafter, he was like Paul Revere sounding an alarm in speeches to garden clubs and civic groups across Texas.

The restoration was to save a building McCree often referred to as "Texas' secular cathedral." He explained it this way: "It's different from any other state, the way Texans feel about their history, their background and their heritage …This unique building symbolizes that."

McCree set a personal deadline: obtain the plans, find

Reflections

Almost from the time he became an Austin firefighter in 1948,
Brady Pool was fascinated by the Capitol.

Like no other Austin building, it had a fire alarm wired directly to the central fire station, a ticker-tape contraption. In his spare time, Pool pored over old log books that contained details of previous Capitol fires, and even found a silver megaphone in a dusty fire station attic that had been used in fighting one such blaze. He studied an old photo showing a horse-drawn steamer engine parked near the burning Capitol.

On February 6, 1983, his curiosity became prophetic. Pool clearly recalls the words of the dispatcher who summoned him from his home: "Working fire in the state Capitol … They've got some fire showing."

It soon was apparent after Pool, the acting fire chief, sped to the scene and crawled on his belly into the burning east wing, that this was the Big One.

Hours later, the efforts of Pool and 118 other firefighters paid off. The three-alarm tragedy had come close to destroying the Capitol. "Absolutely, very close," Pool said.

The Lone Star of Texas atop the inner dome is gold-painted metal; the turn-of-the-century version was painted onto the ceiling surface.

The toll was high: One person died, eleven firefighters and police officers were injured and damage topped $2.5 million. Three people, including the lieutenant governor's daughter, were rescued. A faulty television was blamed.

A succession of official warnings about the Capitol fire danger had begun seventy years earlier, a few years after the first recorded fire damaged a judge's third-floor office in 1904. Complaints about faulty wiring, empty extinguishers, inadequate water hydrants and a junk-filled basement had been heard over and over. Even humorist Will Rogers championed the issue when he addressed the Legislature in 1931: "Everything's going to get burned up if you don't do something. You could at least shellac it."

In 1936, the agency responsible for the Capitol, in a report detailing numerous hazards, called the building "the biggest firetrap in the world." While a restoration was proposed and then scuttled as too expensive, a legislative committee warned: "Should this building be destroyed by fire, priceless archives, records and data would be destroyed, and the members of the Legislature would stand convicted of negligence in failing to recognize the conditions that surround them."

For some, the legacy of that 1983 fire may be the restored Capitol itself. But for firefighters like Pool, it is what is behind the newly redone interiors: fire sprinklers in every room, a computerized alarm system, special design features that will contain smoke and the spread of flames.

Pool, now retired, knows those safety measures mean "the Capitol now won't be the horror story it once was." ★

the money and begin the construction by 1991, when Clements' term would end. Who knew if Clements' successor would be as committed to the project?

So with a revival preacher's zeal, McCree conducted weekly "deficiency tours" for lawmakers to highlight the numerous hazards — leaky pipes, toxic asbestos insulation, cobbled-up wiring — and sell them on the project. On one rainy day, shocked lawmakers watched in the Capitol attic as a bucket brigade of janitors, armed with plastic pails, scrambled to catch a deluge of drips while the House deliberated below.

In 1991, as the restoration project got under way, Texas' most famous silhouette took on a boxy shape after it was completely enshrouded in scaffolding.

Lawmakers were quickly convinced. With little controversy, the Legislature approved nearly $150 million, in cash, to ensure that this time the restoration would be done right.

The Capitol's return to its turn-of-the-century grandeur would mean space for only about a third of the Legislature.

What to do with those lawmakers who could not be housed in the Capitol posed a big problem. The solution proved to be the biggest hole ever dug in Central Texas.

Reflections

*Eddie Yocham, a husky rock cutter from Bertram, Texas,
had quarried tons of limestone during his career, but never
at a job site like this: beneath the Texas Capitol.*

In what surely was the restoration project's engineering feat, Yocham and his employees carved two tunnels out of solid rock, one atop the other, from the Capitol's north steps to the Rotunda. The tunnels link the old building with the new underground extension.

The work was done inside what looked like a mine shaft — dusty rail tracks on the floor, flickering light bulbs, jagged rock walls, steel beams overhead.

Even though Yocham was confident, it was an undertaking that proved the most worrisome for the project's engineers. An unexpected miscue could have collapsed part of the revered building.

Everything went as planned, down to the inch.

The workers carved out space for the tunnels and also new elevator shafts. Polished and painted finishes today give little hint of what once was referred to by hard-hats as "The Mine."

Every step of the work was monitored continuously by sophisticated electronic gadgetry, the kinds of gauges and sensors used in earthquake zones.

Wyatt Graham and Tomas Lorea monitor an automated cutting saw, on track at center, as it slices through solid limestone beneath the Capitol, during construction of the twin tunnels that link the statehouse to the Extension.

Had the building moved even the slightest bit, a yellow warning light at the end of the mine shaft would have flashed and all work would have been halted. Fortunately, the light never signaled trouble.

Two rock saws, resembling huge gray chainsaws on wheels, were used to cut the tunnels. Cutting three feet deep, at a rate of up to one and one-half inches per minute, the saws opened a cavernous hole beneath the statehouse's north basement hallway. As in a quarry, the sawed rock was cut lengthwise, broken into two-foot-by-two-foot blocks and hauled out.

The saw's blade was a lime-green plastic belt, a few inches wide, with diamond-studded steel plates on one side. As the saws cut, their blades were cooled by water, two thousand gallons hourly, all recycled through holding ponds outside.

It was a far cry from the way the Capitol basement had been dug a century earlier. Holes had been pounded into the rock with a hammer and a "star drill," a rod-like tool with cutting edges on the bottom. Then black powder had been poured into the holes before the rock was blasted. Several of those "shot holes" were uncovered in the rock as Yocham's crews cut the new tunnels.

The difference, however, was that those early workers did not have a huge granite building sitting atop their job site. ★

recalled from a sketchbook by a member of the design team.

From the start, money was a key concern. Even after the funding was approved, project officials feared for months that the Legislature might renege because of growing budget woes.

The solution, Keahey recalls: "Commit the project by digging the hole."

It was a big gamble. The blueprints for the building were not even completed. As construction director David Stauch later would explain, "We dug a hole ... The building had to fit in it."

But first, archaeologists culled more than 400,000 artifacts from the tannish soil. And seventeen sprawling oak trees were relocated temporarily into large wooden boxes that were clustered at the edge of the construction site.

The excavation began in May, 1990. Seven months later the sixty-foot-deep chasm was complete, the result of an around-the-clock effort that was halted only once. On the morning of

With skylight-topped Light Courts, designers ensured that most offices in the underground building had daylight. The decorative wall patterns were made from castings of granite features on the Capitol's exterior.

Buried so as not to block the view of the historic Capitol, the Extension covers roughly four blocks north of the statehouse. Only the copper-roofed elevator lobbies and skylights hint of the four-story structure below. Some 680,000 tons of rock were chiseled from the ground to make way for the Extension.

November 28, the Texas Supreme Court met in an adjacent building to hear lawyers' arguments about equality in funding for public schools. For that historic hearing, the noise and vibration stopped.

The sides of the hole had been specially engineered, smoothly cut with a huge, diamond-bladed saw normally used in rock quarries; this would enable the building to fit snugly inside. Everything was ready for construction to start.

Then disaster struck.

The initial bid for the Capitol restoration phase of the project far exceeded the budget. State officials faced this quandary: Build the underground building, for which they had enough money, or stop the entire project and leave the huge pit empty.

Stauch remembers that someone joked that the pit could be filled with water, thereby creating a big lake which could bear the name of the unfortunate official who would get the blame. When lawmakers filed into the hole for a photo, some joked: "Keep an eye on the edges... Make sure the (dump) trucks aren't backed up."

But Stauch and others working on this once-in-a-lifetime job to save Texas' crown jewel of government buildings were not laughing. Those were bleak, soul-searching days for project officials and the designers.

The decision came down to a dramatic vote. In December, 1990, members of the State Preservation Board, the agency in charge of the Capitol work, gave the go-ahead to build the underground structure. The vote would be among the last official decisions for Clements and Lt. Gov. Bill Hobby, both members of the board.

Finding the additional money needed to complete the project would be left to their successors. The gambit worked. Gov. Ann Richards and the Legislature found the money to finish the project.

On January 11, 1993, when a royal blue ribbon was snipped to dedicate the underground building, the dream was finally a reality. The subterranean edifice — $63.9 million worth of concrete and steel and glass and wood in two levels of offices and two of parking — was larger than the Capitol itself. Yet

Brass railings cascade between floors on the twin stairs that flank the Central Court. Flowing architectural lines and repetitive patterns are a hallmark of the building, which has won design accolades. It is as if a fortune cookie message used as an optimistic guide by the Houston-based design team came true: "Success in the end eclipses mistakes along the way."

Reflections

For Victor and Robert Longo, there was a sense of dèjá vu.

Their father had worked on the installation of the Capitol's colorful terrazzo floors, a project commemorating the Texas Centennial in 1936. Now, fifty-five years later, they laid new terrazzo floors in the Capitol Extension, in designs much like those their father had worked on in the old statehouse.

"(The crew) knew that this was probably a once-in-a-lifetime installation … and they wanted to leave something that was going to be of some value, some pride — like the generation before them had done," explained Robert.

The result is the colorful flooring in the underground building; shades of red, green, beige and gray twist and swirl through the hallways in over 56,700 square feet of flowing designs.

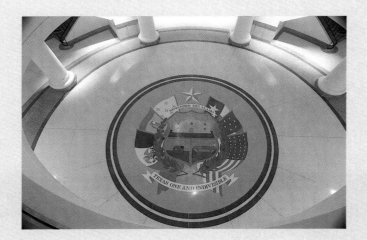

The centerpiece is the reverse of Texas' state seal, displayed in the Seal Court, a design that is seventeen feet wide and features twenty-seven colors. Like the famous terrazzo floor in the Capitol Rotunda, where the six seals of Texas are displayed in vivid color, the reverse seal is an eye-catcher.

The work by the Longos' Houston company took fifteen months, starting in 1991, when workers measured grids on the bare concrete floors of the unfinished building. As a sand and cement underbed was laid, brass dividers were imbedded to form the geometric patterns. After the underbed had dried, workers began laying the floor, using a thin coat of colored cement with matching marble chips mixed in. Starting at the north end of the lower floor, the artisans worked one color and one area at a time until they had covered all floors.

The Seal Court floor features the six flags under which Texas has been governed and a three-part shield depicting icons of the Texas War for Independence: the Alamo, a cannon used in the Battle of Gonzales and Vince's Bridge, a timber crossing destroyed by Texas fighters to thwart advancing Mexican troops.

After the colored cement dried thoroughly, special machines were brought in to grind the surface smooth and polish it.

Work on the seal was the most demanding. The numerous colors in small spots required the detail of an intricate painting, Victor Longo said in an interview before his death in 1994, months after the job was completed. The tiny eye of the eagle on the Mexican flag was made from a single chip, carefully ground down into the right shape.

Throughout the job, precision was a must. "It would show up like a sore thumb if you didn't have it right," said Robert.

The result, he said, is among the most striking design elements of the Capitol Extension — award-winning work produced by hands with, as Robert explains, "a couple, three hundred years' experience." ✭

the Extension was buried, out of view beneath a landscaped plaza, the largest such underground expansion of any state capitol.

The building was completed in two and one-half years, approximately six months less than it took to finish the basement of the Capitol in the 1880s, when only hand tools and dynamite were used.

Not even a series of leaks, reminiscent of the leaky roof during the Capitol's 1888 dedication ceremonies, could dampen the praise for the subterranean showplace.

A new nickname quickly stuck: "The Taj-Ma-Hole."

Above: *Glass railings, thick columns and broad, curving stairways are signatures of the Seal Court, flanked by a dining room and auditorium. Ahead is one of the two tunnels that link the Extension with the Capitol.*
Pages 34 and 35: *Above a constellation of Lone Stars that decorate the railings and sides of the Central Court, an azure Texas sky crowns the view.*

*Th*e pay was just twenty-five cents an hour on a graveyard shift. Occasionally there were rats to contend with, big ones that scurried up and down the pipes in the basement.

But J.J. "Jake" Pickle, Austin's longtime congressman, remembers it as a great job. In 1933, Pickle, then a college sophomore, worked as a night watchman in the Texas Capitol.

Every hour on the hour, Pickle made his rounds of the first floor and basement with a time-clock device dangling from a strap around his neck. At each stop, he inserted a key into the device to record that everything was safe and sound.

Mostly, that nothing was afire.

To him, it was an awesome responsibility, making sure that the corridors of power, probably the most famous hallways in the state, were all right.

Pickle took it seriously. At age seventeen, on his first visit to the Capitol, the boy from Big Spring had stood in awe: "I thought: This is my government, the biggest building I've ever seen."

Standing in the Rotunda, one could get a sense

Corridors of Power

of the bigness of Texas. In each direction, almost as far as the eye could see, hallways stretched into the distance. Their high ceilings gave the feeling of wide open spaces.

Above soared the dome, taller by several feet than the nation's Capitol in Washington. It was not as high as the West Texas sky, but for a building, the feeling seemed just as expansive.

Decorative, huge cast-iron columns forged by convicts in East Texas and frilly plasterwork sculpted by artisans lined each hallway, adding an air of importance. Clearly, these were spaces built

Above: *Cherry wood handrails and a cast-iron balustrade of one of the Capitol's two grand staircases roll between floors.*
Facing page: *Colorful terrazzo flooring commemorating twelve battles in Texas' War for Independence were installed in 1936 in the South Foyer as a Centennial project.*

Soft light from the South Foyer highlights intricate plasterwork and wood detail around doors, seen through one of two passageways that lead to the Rotunda.

as grand passageways to power.

Pickle sometimes would stop on his nighttime rounds to talk to the marble statues of Stephen F. Austin and Sam Houston. "Old fella, you just don't know how tough it is in these days," he would say of the Great Depression. "You think it was tough in your time."

The Capitol was much different then than it is now. In the hallways, where the famous terrazzo designs now lie, there were encaustic tiles arranged in geometric designs, tones of brown, cream and blue. And in the Rotunda, instead of the colorful terrazzo floor depicting the seals of six governments of Texas, there was a glass block floor with a brass star at the center. The blocks allowed natural light to filter into a rotunda in the basement where, looking up during the day, visitors could see shadows moving across the floor above.

While in college, working as a night watchman, former U.S. Rep. J.J. "Jake" Pickle got in trouble for racing his bicycle down Capitol corridors.

The terrazzo on the first floor came two years later, in 1936, as part of a project commemorating the Texas Centennial. Seeking to honor the Texas spirit, artisans arranged chips of marble quarried at various Texas sites into a memorial that covered the South Foyer — the names of twelve battles of the Texas revolution, each with an emblem of crossed torches to represent victory. In the 1950s, as part of a modernization project, terrazzo also was added to the Capitol's upper floors.

Still vivid to Pickle are the clack-clack-clacking sounds that people made as they walked across the old tile. Those sounds are memorable for another reason: He got in trouble in his watchman's job for racing a bicycle down the empty halls, from

Once obscured by makeshift offices and electrical transformers, the basement Rotunda is again a focal point of the long hallways. The ceiling originally was glass-block tiles that were part of the floor of the Rotunda upstairs.

one end of the Capitol to the other. "We'd be an unguided missile coming through that Rotunda," he says.

If the first floor was memorable for its design touches, the basement was another story. It contained offices, work rooms for repairing typewriters and such, and storage rooms. Most were full with cardboard boxes of old records, visible through wire-grille doors in the thick walls. The floors were cold, gray concrete.

But at night, when the Capitol was deadly quiet, Pickle sometimes found the basement a haven.

If Pickle was late in making his rounds, Pickle's supervisor — "a great, kind old gentleman," he recalls — would come looking for him. "He'd come up the basement [hallway] and always clear his throat real loud a hundred yards away so he'd be sure I was awake... He never caught me asleep because he'd always wake me up."

In later years, the storage rooms filled with offices. Halls were narrowed. Rows of stately cast-iron columns and the basement Rotunda disappeared behind artless wood paneling.

Only now, sixty years after Pickle worked there, has the subterranean space been returned to its original grandeur.

If there is a single symbol of the Capitol, it is the dome, a rounded cap that would have been square, like a clock tower, had the original design been carried out. Were the dome a hat, it would be the state's most famous bowler, a silhouette featured on everything from newspaper mastheads to plumbing trucks to cans of coffee, even chocolate candy — familiar to a century of Texans.

From the day the Capitol opened in May 1888, the dome and Rotunda have been the building's most awe-inspiring features, big and grand places in a building with the same virtues. They are much-storied places, as well. And even the tall tales about them demonstrate much about how Texas views itself: One story boasts that the Washington Monument could stand upright inside the Rotunda without ever touching the ceiling, even though the Monument is more than two hundred feet higher than the statehouse. Only Texans would make such a claim.

If the famous view from the center of the Rotunda, looking up to the Lone Star in the dome's apex, has been special, so has the dome's uppermost limits.

Count Jim Mattox, former state attorney general and former member of the Texas House and U.S. Congress, among the fans.

"I have purposely climbed as high as one can climb in the Capitol dome, even up to where the lights are. Maybe it's the kid in me that says that I want to have been to the top.

"There's nothing more beautiful than ... at Christmas season, to look out over the downtown Christmas lights and to see the real majesty of the city from that vantage point."

It was 1973, just after he was elected to

Below: Paintings of former governors watch over the second floor of the Rotunda. Brass railing is not original to the building, but was required by modern safety codes.
Pages 42 and 43: Graceful curves of arches, decorative plasterwork and columns are bathed in afternoon light in the East Lobby.

*Above: Arms of the grand staircase wind to a lower-floor landing. **Facing page:** Like soldiers lined up in a row, stair railings march in formation between floors. Each is painted bronze green with highlights tinted in gold-colored paint.*

the Texas House, that Mattox made the first of more than two dozen trips to the top, up the spindly and narrow spiral staircase that hangs from one side of the inner dome. Public tours to that part of the dome were halted years ago because of safety concerns. Amid the dust and debris, the dome became mostly a place for pigeons and other birds.

But Mattox kept going back, borrowing the key from Capitol police while he was a lawmaker and later the attorney general. On his last trip a few years ago, Mattox found "a small hawk that was up there and I did my best to catch him."

Just as the dome is special to Mattox, so has it been to Texas. In the early 1920s, when state officials painted the outside white, there was immediate public outrage. Within months it was repainted its traditional stone color.

For generations the dome has been a beacon for travelers coming to Austin, a signature of the city that is visible from miles away even at night. That scene is so revered that it is protected by a law that restricts the height of new buildings

Reflections

The boys made Thelma Bills Anderson do it.

In 1931, while serving as the first female page in the Texas Senate, Anderson tiptoed around the Rotunda atop the second-floor handrail, a breathtaking stunt she never forgot. Or ever repeated.

Then a pert thirteen-year-old, she was dared by the boy pages; it was a rite of passage, perhaps, as a Capitol custom was broken. "I was challenged all the time," she recalls. But most of the dares were for things such as mumbletypeg and other boys' games.

Even now, the details of that short walk remain clear to Anderson — the narrow rail, just 11 inches wide, its shiny and sloping top. The tile and glass-block floor below seemed miles away. Far enough, surely, for a fatal fall, as had occurred just a few years earlier when a hapless painter slipped from scaffolding while touching up the inside of the dome.

Thelma Bills Anderson by the Rotunda railing she once walked. The brass rail atop it was added years later.

She was an unlikely daredevil. Growing up just a block from the Capitol, Anderson found that her several trips to the top of the dome were "quite scary" because of the height. But on the day she walked the Rotunda railing, those fears were forgotten.

Once she proved to the boys that she could do it, Anderson said she never wanted to repeat the stunt. "I don't even like to walk out on that section any more," she said.

Years later, when she visited the Capitol with her children, "I wouldn't even let them look over the banister. I made them get back and look through the spokes, it made me so nervous."

She has other Capitol memories: the deep-pile carpet and the colorful characters in the Senate, the state library where she could travel across the country by reading out-of-town newspapers, the foul-smelling drinking fountains, the musty basement and the pond on the west grounds that was filled with big goldfish.

"I loved the statuary by Elisabet Ney and I loved to read the documents. I was always impressed by the ring of governors (paintings)" on the walls of the Rotunda.

Her interest in being a page, she said, was piqued by the election of Miriam "Ma" Ferguson in 1925 as the first woman governor, and Margie Neal of Carthage in 1927 as the first woman senator. "It was a trend … I got a bug in my mind," she said.

It was a trend that did not last, as far as Senate pages went. The next female page was not appointed until the 1970s. ★

in several so-called "view corridors." Unfortunately, the law came too late to save some of the treasured vistas.

It is a view George Christian knows well. He grew up around the Capitol. His father served as an appellate judge there, his mother worked as a clerk in the comptroller's office, and he worked as a reporter and gubernatorial press secretary in the 1940s and 1950s.

One view, from a spot he was attracted to as a child, holds fond memories: "I liked to climb up to the dome … It was challenging to get up there and look down at the Rotunda because the Rotunda had a star in it at that time. It looked like a Texas Ranger badge. And kids loved it."

Though the star is long gone, replaced by a terrazzo floor in 1936, the special aura of the statehouse remains unchanged. Christian, an Austin political consultant who served as press secretary to President Lyndon Johnson, thinks the Capitol has been charmed since its construction:

"We could be whatever we want to be. We are the biggest state. We have the richest traditions. We look after ourselves. If anybody messes with us, we swat them in the teeth. That was the heritage.

"We were self-reliant. We knew how to get things done. When we didn't have enough money to build the dadgum thing, we traded around until we could get a deal… Couldn't do it any other way. We did a deal. And would that have happened somewhere else? I doubt it.

Above: Victorian and Neo-Classic lines of the statehouse are evident in this view of the Rotunda, showing three of its four levels. *Pages 48 and 49:* From the fourth floor, the Rotunda is a study in curves and contrasting colors and lights. Portraits on walls are chief executives of Texas, in order, ascending from the first floor.

Reflections

*Late at night the deserted Capitol hallways fill with a soft stillness,
a contemplative and enticing quiet that can nurture special
thoughts about Texas history, amid the grand architecture.*

It was here that John and Nell Connally came in January 1963, after he was elected governor, to look and to admire. And to think.

A marble bust of Texas' first female governor, Miriam "Ma" Ferguson, sits beneath the painting of a predecessor, Albert C. Horton, who was acting governor in 1846 and 1847.

Through the legislative chambers they wandered, up and down the shadowy halls and into the Rotunda where just a day earlier they had stood for hours, greeting and shaking hands with thousands of Texans who had come to the inauguration.

"You wonder about those other people who have passed through those halls and who have served in those rooms and it's just a very historical time," Mrs. Connally remembered thinking. "It was exciting and thrilling and scary and wonderful. (Scary) because you want to be sure that you do what you were elected to do, and this is the place of business."

In many ways, she said, the nighttime tour "helped us just reinforce our desire to do good things for the State of Texas that we love."

After their stroll was finished, they returned to the Governor's Mansion across the street. But Mrs. Connally's special feelings about the statehouse remained.

In 1988, she returned to a lavishly decorated statehouse, as chairwoman of a Capitol Centennial celebration that saw 800 invited guests served a catered dinner in the same hallways the Connallys once had walked.

"Down both those wings to the right and left were round tables for 400 on each side ... and then we had the orchestra and dancing in the Rotunda," she said. "It was a beautiful evening."

Just as the Capitol meant happy times for the Connallys, it also marked sad ones. After John Connally died in 1993, his body lay in state in the House Chamber before the funeral at a nearby church.

In a way, it was as if the Capitol once again was a peaceful and calm place for the Connallys, just like that night in 1963 when they explored its quietude. ✮

"It says we're different. We're as good as the U.S. of A., and we're part of the U.S. of A. and proud of it. But boy, they don't have anything on us. Our Capitol is... taller than theirs.

"It's a symbol of greatness, size, power. Everybody can take pride in that, even when they live in a shack."

Above: Long ago removed to make way for office space, the stairway at the east end of the basement has been returned. Thick walls are typical in basement spaces.
Pages 52 and 53: *Patterned after the U.S. Capitol, the inner dome rises majestically above the Rotunda. At right is a spiral staircase leading to the top. A large, 25-light chandelier once hung far into the Rotunda from the star.*

*F*rom the time Emil Stryk stepped into the Treasury Office in 1935, as a new bookkeeper making $131 a month, he knew it was someplace special.

Just inside the south door of the Capitol, the cashier's office looked more like a jail than the bank it was. It had shiny bars of chrome steel stretching from floor to ceiling, inset with teller windows. Adjacent to the office was a double-decked vault, a Fort Knox of Texas. The vault stored the state's riches, millions of dollars in cash, bonds and securities.

In time, Stryk even would do duty on what may have been the most unusual job in the Capitol: sleeping outside the vault as a human alarm system, a practice that continued until the Treasury Office moved from the Capitol in 1971.

"I probably slept there three, maybe four Christmases before the Second World War, two or three days usually, while the fellow whose job that was went home to see his people," says

Silver and Steel

Stryk, now in his eighties.

Had anything ever happened, he was there to sound an alarm. He never had to.

Little wonder. Stryk, who later would manage the important vault during his forty-one years as a Treasury employee, knew that the place was one of the most secure in Austin. The vault was one of eighteen built in the new statehouse, mostly to protect valuable records from fire. But as originally planned, the Treasury's twin vault was the king.

It was to be made of brick-encased stones fastened together with two-inch metal rods

Above: Victorian-edged door transom marks the Treasury office entry.
Facing page: Gently curving bars of chrome steel again encircle the State Treasury office, one of the most dramatic of the restored rooms. Pages 56 and 57: Distinctive bars and checkerboard floor mark the restored Treasury office.

Solemn Treasury employees paused for this early 1890s photo inside the Treasury's barred office. The calendar on the wall at left says "The Big Texas House."

made from cannon shot. The interior was lined with slabs of granite up to ten inches thick, each locked into the stonework with iron anchors. Space between the exterior and interior walls was to be filled with broken glass and chips of stone.

In the weeks after the statehouse was dedicated in 1888, newspapers touted the security of the vault. The *Austin Daily Statesman* called it, "a tremendous chrome steel money vault."

A new vault built in 1936, buried just west of the Capitol's south wing, adjacent to its foundation wall and connected to the basement, was no less secure. Its concrete walls were twenty-eight inches thick; its door weighed twenty-eight tons. It was built with a walkway around its perimeter to deter tunneling thieves.

But the precautions paid off. There were no reports of thieves successfully penetrating those two Capitol vaults.

When H. Morris Stevens joined the Treasury as a clerk in 1936, he was quickly impressed with the surroundings and working conditions. His job paid more than three times what he had been making as a shoe salesman during the Great Depression. Like Stryk, he quickly sized up the place as one of the safest in Austin, perhaps even in Texas.

Inside the vaults was enough cash to operate the state and millions of dollars' worth of bonds, said Stevens, who later would become chief clerk during a forty-six-year career with the agency.

Stories abounded about how the Treasury had once been robbed, and how the Capitol vaults had been specially strengthened to make sure that never happened again. True or not, Stevens never doubted the state's money was safe and sound in the vaults.

Despite the precautions inside the Capitol, Stevens

Restored counter area appears much the same as it did years ago. The room is now the Capitol information desk.

Reflections

As a young boy growing up in Austin, B.L. Westlund was fascinated by the Capitol. Thirty years ago, his admiration having carried into his adulthood, for a few dollars he bought an old chair from the statehouse.

It was something with which he could remember the grand old building.

Now, it has come home, back to its original place in a legislative chamber.

"It just kind of gives me a good feeling," he said.

He is not alone in his sentiment.

From across Texas, out of dusty attics and dingy storage rooms, people returned an assortment of Capitol furniture and artifacts while the restoration project was under way — each piece contributing to the historic project.

Austinite Helen Eby Craig, who donated a walnut Senate chair in 1993, explained: "They're restoring the Capitol. I wanted them to have it."

Bonnie Campbell, the Capitol curator, attributes the interest to Texans' affection for the building — and the project itself.

"As people see that, even though they're very attached to some of these (furniture) items, it seems like the right thing to do is to give it back to the Capitol where it will be cared for and preserved forever," she said.

Westlund's swivel chair was one of more than 100 used in the House chamber from 1889 until the 1940s. Since then, most swivels had been disposed of and only a few remained in state possession.

It was made by the Milwaukee Chair Company, one of three chair makers who helped furnish the pink-granite Capitol after it was completed in 1888.

Among old business machines inside the Treasury office is this typewriter, one of many donated antiques now a part of the historic furnishings collection.

One arm had been broken off Westlund's oak chair years ago, but he kept the pieces, always intending to restore it. Officials completed the job, including a leather seat and a backrest just like it had originally.

Now, a few of those statehouse artifacts are carefully displayed throughout the Capitol in proper settings so that tour guides can explain how the Capitol looked years ago, from chairs to an old typewriter that sits on the Treasury Office counter.

In all, more than 800 pieces of original Capitol furniture are among more than 2,000 historic items and artwork in the Capitol Collection. ✯

recalls that in the 1930s he and another Treasury employee carried sizable sums of cash — as much as $100,000 — in sacks up Congress Avenue from local banks to the Capitol. And, he insists, it occurred on more than one occasion, without incident.

The old Treasury vault in the Capitol basement was installed in 1936, and is encircled by a security walkway. The door weighs 28 tons.

In the early 1950s, to save the expense of using armored cars, Stevens recalls that he and Treasurer Jesse James transferred $60 million in government bonds between the Capitol and the Federal Reserve Bank in San Antonio in three Department of Public Safety cars, with Texas Rangers riding shotgun.

In 1909, officials of the Waters-Pierce Oil Company, found guilty of antitrust violations, paid a $1.8 million fine at the Treasury Office — in cash. At the time, it was the largest penalty ever collected against a U.S. corporation.

The money arrived in a car, surrounded by armed guards who escorted it from two downtown banks and up Congress Avenue to the Capitol's front door, in what became known as Austin's "Million-Dollar Parade." Along with bank offi-

Reflections

As a high school junior, sightseeing while in Austin for a debate tournament, L. DeWitt Hale toured the Capitol for the first time in 1933. And he never forgot the feeling. So massive, so strong, so impressive, he recalls.

Above: *Weighing 12,000 pounds, the Capitol's cornerstone was laid in place on March 2, 1885.*

Facing page: *Capitol tour guides huddle where millions of dollars in cash and bonds once were kept, inside one of the Treasury office's vaults.*

There were the grand ceilings, the towering Rotunda, the huge dome and the massive wooden doors with the solid brass hinges, the ones imprinted with the words "Texas Capitol." Even though he knew little of the building's history, everything about the statehouse indicated strength to the young Hale.

It was just what the Capitol's planners had wanted.

Generally patterned after the U.S. Capitol in Washington in style and size, state officials had built this Capitol to last — a massive, cut stone foundation and foot-thick limestone walls in the interior, all from stone that was blasted and chiseled by hand from quarries in Burnet County and near Oatmanville, southwest of Austin.

Built into those walls was much history. Hundreds of convicts quarried the stone, and Scottish stonecutters were imported to do the finishing work.

Nonetheless, Hale never forgot those initial feelings, even as he returned to the Capitol in 1939 as a twenty-one-year-old state representative from Collin County, the youngest member to have served.

Not until the 1950s, Hale recalls, when he returned to the House after an absence of a few years, did he come to see that strength first-hand, during a project to add two new elevators just north of the Rotunda.

"I'm telling you, the biggest problem there was was going through those walls... about a foot thick," remembers Hale, who now lives in Austin. "It would take an atom bomb to knock this building down, the way it was built.'

It is a place, he says, as solid as Texas. ★

cials, the entourage reportedly included the district judge before whom the case was tried, the county attorney, the sheriff, a Texas Ranger, the attorney general, state treasurer, practically every Austin lawyer that had assisted in the case, and a guard of mounted peace officers. Once at the Capitol, a photographer recorded wide-eyed state officials gathered close around a table where the money was piled high.

But for that windfall, state government that year would have faced a deficit of $347,144.

In 1971, because of crowded working conditions, the Treasury moved into new offices three blocks away. As legislators moved into the emptied space, one area quickly became sought after as offices: the old vaults.

Below: In August 1909, after hauling $1,808,483.30 to the Capitol in a heavily guarded car, officials posed with the money before it went into the vault. The cash was a court-ordered fine paid by an oil company. ***Facing page:*** Now an object of curiosity by passersby, this old office machine stands at one end of the restored Treasury office.

*Th*is desk could be no ordinary desk. It had to be elaborate, something big and grand.

The year was 1888, and Texas had just completed its new Capitol. The pink granite building was touted as the seventh largest in the world, bigger than life, at least as big as Texas thought of itself.

And this desk had to reflect that it was for the governor, the chief executive of a state that considered itself an equal to foreign nations — a person who, like royalty, was sometimes addressed as "your excellency."

The new desk did just that. It was made of fine mahogany, not oak or walnut like other Capitol desks. It had elaborate carvings on its drawer fronts, ornate brass handles, a delicate rail along its top, even a mirror hidden behind a small panel.

A fine piece of furniture it was. So fine, in fact, that Marshall Field, the Chicago retail king,

Place of Grand Dreams

had one like it — only his was oak, not the richer mahogany.

It was the centerpiece of the governor's small private office, an oasis of finery tucked into the Capitol's south wing, just off the first-floor foyer. In an adjacent room was the Governor's Business Office, occupied by clerks and functionaries who toiled at cheaper walnut desks.

Just outside the private office, up a narrow

Above: A brass eagle maintains its silent vigil atop the flagstaff in the Governor's Public Reception Room. **Facing page:** *The room was the most opulent of any in the Capitol, a Victorian parlor that featured expensive design touches and furnishings. It was the only Capitol room that received cherry wood trim and wainscoting.*

The original governor's desk is visible, although cluttered, in this circa-1901 photograph of the chief executive's private office on the first floor. Seated at right is Gov. Samuel Willis Tucker Lanham, with an unidentified man. Note the spittoon on the floor and the candlestick telephone on the table at left.

spiral staircase and on the second floor, were the remaining gubernatorial offices: two small offices designated as "consultation rooms," places that some governors would use as secret hideaways.

Adjacent was the spacious Public Reception Room, by far the most luxurious area in the Capitol.

An elaborate Victorian parlor, it was decorated with mahogany furniture, cherry woodwork, colorful carpets and cascading draperies that cost at least three times as much as any others in the building. A brass chandelier shimmered from the high ceiling and in one corner, on its own pedestal, glistened a silver-plated water pitcher and mug.

Nearby was a plush couch made famous by President William McKinley's wife who, by some accounts, sought respite there during a faint spell. She remarked that it had no pillows; as a thank-you gesture, she sent a large square pillow made of lavender silk as a gift to Texas. It remained on the couch for years, or so the story goes.

Indeed, these were grand digs for a job that drew great and legendary men, a place once referred to as "Texas' parlor of kings."

The first to use the offices was Lawrence "Sul" Ross, former Texas Ranger, Indian fighter, Confederate general who had seven horses shot out from beneath him during battle, tough frontier sheriff who helped tame "Six-Shooter Junction," as Waco was once known.

His life story reads like Western legend, the stuff of which little boys dream, in a state heading from the Wild West to a new century.

Texas was changing. And the governor's desk, unlike others in the Capitol, was the setting for much of that history.

It was here that governors signed legislation that created the Texas Railroad Commission and Texas Tech University. Prisons and schools were reformed, several times. The decision to grant women the right to vote was made here. With his signature, a governor dispatched Texas troops to capture Mexican bandit Pancho Villa.

In the Reception Room, William Jennings Bryan, the silver-tongued orator, shook more than five thousand hands during a 1907 reception. President Theodore Roosevelt had greeted dignitaries here two years earlier. Upon their respective deaths, the bodies of three former governors lay in state here.

In 1917, through the open window of his first-floor office, Gov. Jim "Pa" Ferguson watched as angry University of Texas supporters protested his veto of the school's appropriation. Their anger, plus allegations that he misused state money, would later lead to his impeachment.

During those years, the offices changed little, except for an occasional sprucing up. But by the time the Roaring Twenties began, the office was no longer grand enough.

Intricate carved doors and a delicate top rail decorate the original governor's desk. Note the unusual swirl-design carpet, replicated to look like the original floor covering from old photographs and extensive research.

Reflections

As Capitol sights go, the spot was nothing fancy. It was just a gray marble-backed niche in a south foyer wall, the site of an abandoned drinking fountain. Had it not been near an elevator, most passersby might have missed it.

But it was a special place for Gov. Dolph Briscoe. In the niche, behind a wrought-iron grille, was a copy of Texas' Declaration of Independence from Mexico. The last signature was that of his forefather, Andrew Briscoe.

During his years at the Capitol, Briscoe stopped there many times — to look, and to think.

"That took a lot of courage for those people back in that day to put everything they had — including their lives — on the line, which is what they did, in order to try and make an independent nation out of Texas. If it hadn't worked, they would've all been killed."

"That was inspirational to me … It serves as an inspiration to try my best to figure out the right thing to do and then have the courage to follow through on it."

The document was put on display in 1929. Across the foyer, in a second niche, was a copy of Texas' 1861 secession from the Union.

As part of the restoration, the water fountains have been returned. And the wrought-iron grilles and the copies of the documents they once protected are in storage, possibly for use in a future history exhibit. ✭

Gov. Pat Neff, in 1922, redecorated the offices. The huge desk ended up in the Capitol basement, from where it was almost auctioned in 1929.

The governor's private office moved upstairs into one of the consultation rooms just off the Reception Room.

That would be a place where Texas' first woman governor, Miriam "Ma" Ferguson, and its youngest, Dan Moody, age thirty-three, would work. "Ma" once remarked that Moody's selection as her successor, in 1927, was "about as novel as my election as a woman governor. Time alone will prove whether the people have acted wisely in either case."

By the early 1930s, the Great Depression had left Texas reeling. The state budget was bleeding red ink, thousands were on relief and the economy was shot. Being governor was a thankless job.

By 1933, the Reception Room, its grandeur a bit shopworn, had become a relief headquarters.

It was during that period that Dolph Briscoe first visited the Capitol. His father was a friend of Gov. Ross Sterling, a Houston business executive who founded the company that

In the foyer outside the Reception Room, arched niches have been restored after being closed in years past so that the Press Room could expand. The door at left leads to a room that was the longtime home of the Texas Railroad Commission, and now serves as a gubernatorial press briefing room. Portraits of the most recent governors were hung here instead of in the Rotunda.

Reflections

Just as the Texas governor's office had character, so did its occupants.

A solemn portrait of former Gov. Ross Sterling is displayed in the Rotunda along those of all other Texas chief executives. The portraits are hung in order starting with the oldest on the first floor.

Former Gov. James "Pa" Ferguson, known for his populist and folksy style, sometimes poked fun at his political rivals with homespun stories. Ferguson was a boyhood inspiration to Preston Smith, who figured, "If he can be governor, why can't I someday?" Smith did, from 1969 to 1973.

Smith recalls this tale from the 1930s, one that Ferguson told about Ross Sterling, one of Ferguson's political rivals.

Smith remembers Ferguson's words:

"When (Sterling) got down to the hunting lodge, he discovered that he forgot his gun. So he called his wife to have her send the gun ... She said, 'I can't understand you. What did you say?' So he said, 'Gun.'

"She said, 'I still can't understand you. Spell it to me.'

"He said, 'G as in Jesus, U as in Europe and N as in pneumonia. Gun!!'" ✭

Its shape a sign of its Victorian roots, this tête-à-tête is among the special furnishings in the Reception Room.

Often used by governors for public events in the Reception Room, this marble-topped table is among the room's historic furnishings.

would later become the oil giant Exxon.

Briscoe, then nine, remembers the thrill of staying overnight at the Governor's Mansion and sleeping in the bed that once belonged to Texas hero Sam Houston. A lasting vision, however, was of the lines of jobless men pleading for the governor's help.

"He could hardly make his way down the walkway," Briscoe recalls. "It did impress me as a little kid that there were that many people looking for jobs. And, of course, there wasn't anything he could do to help them."

Before he left office, Sterling lost his own fortune to the Depression. Forty years later, Briscoe became governor.

In 1939, the office relocated again. "Pappy" Lee O'Daniel, a flamboyant flour salesman known for his folksy live radio broadcasts, frequently used the Reception Room for his office. A five-foot-long conference table served as his desk.

The office moved again in the early 1960s, when John Connally became governor. It moved into a spacious room just east of the Reception Room, an area that originally had been the Capitol post office. A private elevator was installed where the spiral staircase had been.

New gold carpets and draperies also were installed. And a new desk was acquired.

Nearly ten years later, the decor changed again. Briscoe redecorated in red, his wife's favorite color.

While the office had changed dramatically through the years, the aspirations of those who sought it did not. Gov. Preston Smith found his inspiration, reading Jim Ferguson's newspaper when he was just a nine-year-old farmboy in Texas.

"I agreed with a lot of what he had to say ... I thought, if he can be governor, why can't I someday? I knew I wanted to be governor," Smith recalls.

By 1970, twenty-two governors had used the Capitol offices. But the old desk, the place where frontiersman Sul Ross once sat as governor, was virtually forgotten.

That same year the desk was rescued, dusty and rat-gnawed, from a state warehouse at the behest of Ima Hogg, daughter of Gov. James Hogg, the second governor to use it. She arranged for it to be donated to a Brazoria County museum and park that bears Hogg's name.

Joe Cariker, the park superintendent, transported it from Austin in his pickup truck. For $115, he subsequently had it refinished by convicts at an Angleton prison and placed it on display in Hogg's plantation home.

It would be 1993 before Capitol officials, after searching eight years for the desk, finally discovered its whereabouts. A newspaper story had detailed their search as part of the Capitol restoration project.

Delicate carvings like this are featured on the Victorian-era furnishings of the Reception Room.

Still inside the desk drawers were numbers and initials, unexplained inscriptions from the past.

In late 1994, the desk was returned to its original place in the Capitol – in the first-floor private office, restored to its original look.

This time, however, there is a twist. No longer do just great men aspire to the office, but women as well.

THE CAPITOL OF TEXAS

Ann Richards, who in 1990 became the second woman elected governor, likes to imagine a little girl who is thumbing through a textbook. The girl pauses at a photo of Richards among those of Texas' governors.

"See, I can do that someday," the girl exclaims. "I can be governor."

Above: *In an historic portrait, five of the six living governors of Texas posed in the Reception Room before George W. Bush's inauguration in January 1995. From left, Bill Clements, Dolph Briscoe, Bush, Preston Smith and Mark White. According to tradition, Bush's predecessor, Ann Richards, below, was not present.* **Facing page:** *A striking veneer design graces a table in the Governor's Public Reception Room.*

*Th*he Texas Capitol is more than just a building to John Hannah. It is an attitude.

"I think the building was probably designed to make people act heroic," he says. "It certainly has heroic proportions. There certainly have been a lot of heroic acts here."

As secretary of state, Hannah had a special vantage point.

In 1991, Hannah was the 61st secretary to occupy the first-floor Capitol office, a spacious suite with high ceilings, a row of large windows to one side and an imposing two-level vault to the other.

Just a few steps from Hannah's desk was a smaller one that was named for Stephen F. Austin, the so-called father of Texas and secretary of state when Texas was a republic. Austin neither used it nor one like it, but the name stuck anyway. And on the walls were paintings of other Texas heroes that, coupled with the

Stately Business

grand Victorian architecture, warmed the room with a sense of history.

The office of secretary of state is the only executive branch office to have remained in its original Capitol location from the time the building was opened. All the other constitutional officials have moved, even the governor.

Through the years, as the Legislature gobbled up more and more Capitol space, the Senate tried to move the secretary of state, whose staff long ago had expanded into adjacent buildings. But governors, for whom the secretary of

Above: *Laws in these time-worn books were legislated when the Capitol was new.*
Facing page: *A wooden desk, leather-seated swivel chair and replica carpet give the Secretary of State's office the feel of an earlier era.*

state works, refused to sanction the move.

The space still was sought after even as the Capitol restoration project was getting under way.

"The senators ... would drop by after work and have a drink and almost invariably, especially the ones who had been here a long time, you could tell they wanted the secretary of state's office," Hannah recalls.

"You could see them thinking how much space they could have for senators ... They would say, 'Why are you in this building? You have a building. The treasurer has a building; they're out. The land commissioner has a building; he's out. You're the only constitutional office that has an agency that's still in this building.'"

Hannah repeated what many of his predecessors surely had stated: This is where the secretary of state always has been — "I'm supposed to be close to the governor."

He had no intention of leaving this inspirational building.

Almost from the time he was sworn in as a

Above: The table, chairs, marble-backed corner wash basin and mirrored armoire are features of the restored office. ***Below:*** A painting depicts the Alamo, the so-called cradle of Texas liberty. ***Facing page:*** Handwritten extradition records are among the archival files kept in the Secretary of State's office, some in tall metal filing shelves like the ones shown at rear.

Reflections

Dealey Decherd Herndon has called herself "the phenomenon that no one can figure out."

In April 1991, she was hired as executive director of the State Preservation Board. She would be the chief of the complicated Capitol restoration project, even though she had no experience in construction management and no formal training in either architecture or historic preservation.

The Austin resident had been a volunteer in non-profit organizations and had an interest in government and preservation.

Corinthian capital on one of the 110 columns in the statehouse.

But Herndon said she never had any doubt but that she could see the project to a successful completion. This was more than a job for her. It was a labor of love.

"I love the beauty of things that are old and that have been made by hand and have a sense of history to them," she said. "I love the building, not just the architecture of it. I love what it stands for."

Even before she became its chief, Herndon was familiar with the project, having served since 1987 as the citizen member of the Preservation Board. Before that, she had been actively involved in the restoration of the Governor's Mansion, serving as that group's administrator for a year.

She also serves on the board of directors of A.H. Belo Corporation, a Dallas media company that bills itself as the oldest continually operating business in Texas. Her late father had served as chairman of the board.

For Herndon, the Capitol project was history in the making. But there was a personal side, too.

Her grandfather, Ewing Thomason, served in the Capitol as House speaker. Her great grandfather, W.O. Davis, served as a senator during the construction of the Capitol. Her husband, David, was an assistant secretary of state.

"Every time I'm in the building I see crowds of people all fascinated, all looking around ... They all seem to be learning something from it, getting something from it," she says.

"This is an incredible opportunity to give Texas the best Capitol restoration ever." ✮

state representative in January 1967, Hannah said he recognized the Capitol's special aura. His first office "wasn't over four feet by four feet ... I could barely get my desk [in] and I'd almost have to climb over it to get behind it," he recalls.

But the size made him think big.

"It affects the attitudes of the people that work there," Hannah explained. "It makes them realize that people will follow them and ... that they are [just] temporary occupants of the building ...

"It's not their personal place but it is an historical place that belongs to the people of Texas."

In the early 1970s, when Texas government was mired in the Sharpstown influence-peddling scandal, Hannah said he saw his theory about the Capitol's inspiration reinforced. "I think it gave me the courage to do the things that I thought that I needed to do and would have otherwise been reluc-

This circa-1910 view of the Secretary of State's office looks much the same as the restored office does today. Note the revolving bookcase near the desk, and the rugs on top of the carpet.

Through the years, the double-decked vaults in the Secretary of State's Office maintained their original doors and delicate-looking mezzanine stairways.

tant to do," he said.

During that period, Hannah was a member of the so-called "Dirty Thirty," a group of reform-minded House members who challenged — and eventually broke — a House leadership they insisted was autocratic and beholden to special interests.

Hannah said the inspiring experience affected not only him, but others — lawmakers and visiting members of the public alike, who would pack the galleries "to boo the bad guys and cheer the good guys."

Hannah likens the inspirational nature of the Capitol to many federal courtrooms built with the same high ceilings and impressive architecture. A former federal prosecutor, Hannah explains: "Lawyers act differently, judges act differently, juries act differently and witnesses act differently in those huge, impressive courtrooms than they do in small, little courtrooms with low ceilings.

"... It's quieter in those [grand] courtrooms, people are more timid in those courtrooms. People take their business

Inside one of the vaults, where important papers and files once were kept, there is now an office. This one is in one of the two double-decked vaults that flank the Secretary of State's suite, which has retained the same room assignment it had when the Capitol was new.

Reflections

*As a worker pulled off the wooden wainscoting, the deteriorated
postcards tumbled out, six in all. Long hidden inside a Capitol wall,
they were like cryptic pieces of history, intriguing yet enigmatic.*

"If I leave my home for you, can you earn enough for two?" read one. Inside was a large red heart. On another: "Practice makes perfect but be careful what you practice." "Here's champagne to our real friends, and real pain to our sham friends," read one card. Another showed a nude boy grinning, his hands clasped modestly in front of him.

The cards were among a strange collection of artifacts recovered during the Capitol restoration project — items found inside walls, beneath floors, even the date "April 1938" cast into a concrete slab in the basement. The origin of the cards remains a mystery.

The collection of artifacts was discovered in October, 1992, inside the wall and near a window of a third-floor room in the Capitol's north wing, probably a former court office or that of a judge.

These old postcards were among many unexplained artifacts found inside the Capitol during its restoration.

A full-color, German-made card offered the best clues. It showed a grand Victorian home identified only as "residence on Maple Ave., Dallas, Tex." Postmarked Aug. 1, 1910, it carried instructions about depositing money in a bank. It was mailed to a James F. Ewing in Austin, possibly in care of the Court of Criminal Appeals.

A small clipping, a United Press article from Aug. 25 of an unknown year, tells of the second marriage and "automobile honeymoon to New York" of Gypsy Rose Lee, "a former strip-tease dancer" who was famous in the 1930s.

A yellowed cartoon from a newspaper shows a hen on a golf course; its punch line has turned into a fill-in-the-blank puzzle by insects: "Oh! What's the use, —— Everytime I try to hatch —— that fellow comes alo—— drives it into another pla——."

Working beneath the wooden floor in the House Chamber, in an area that was not accessible since the Capitol was built, workers found a pair of women's black dress gloves and a fan.

While removing damaged cornice plaster near a window in the Legislative Reference Library on the second floor, workers discovered a half-moon-shaped piece of wood — part of a plaster barrel lid, probably hidden since before the Capitol was completed in 1888. "Windsor Plaster Mills, Staten Island, N.Y.," reads the red and yellow label. "The celebrated Diamond Brand Plaster. Pure white gypsum plaster was quarried from mines in Nova Scotia."

It is in storage along with the postcards and papers and other treasures, all destined for eventual display in a Capitol history exhibit. ✷

a lot more seriously in huge, imposing, impressive courtrooms.

"You think larger, more grandiose in a large and grandiose room."

And at the Capitol, Hannah believes, there is another effect, as well.

For most officials, he said, their Capitol years tend to be exciting and historic regardless of the small role they may play.

"They thought that what they were doing was going to affect not only them, but other people," he said. "I think that's why people that have been connected with (the Capitol) have some type of awe and fond remembrance of it, because even if you were here and were beaten, or lost some particular thing that you were for, a personal thing happened to you and … probably you were involved in something that was bigger than yourself."

Looking just like Capitol originals, two chairs flank a glass-fronted bookcase.

Reflections

When he was a boy, Roger Joslin imagined he was a fighter at the Alamo in a childhood game that made Texas history seem real.

It was history he and his playmates could almost reach out and touch — the kind of experience, he said, that made him realize that Texas history was not just something one learned, "it was something you belonged to."

As an adult, Joslin touched that history for real.

The East Austin furniture maker built tables for the restored Texas Capitol, custom pieces that look just like the originals from a century ago, right down to the fluted legs and green-cloth tops on some.

Joslin's company was among those in 1994 that replicated original Capitol furniture in order that the rooms of the restored building, though functional for modern state government, could return to their turn-of-the-century style. In cases where original furniture was in bad shape or missing, duplicating it made perfect sense. The originals were well-built, sturdy, functional — and historically correct.

In all, about fifty types of original furniture were replicated, built from scratch down to the tiniest detail. It is, most likely, the biggest such project in Texas.

For the job, Joslin carefully selected white oak and walnut, trying to match the color and grain of the original tables as closely as possible. Every piece was measured and remeasured; each had to duplicate the original in every detail, whether it could be seen or not. In all, Joslin said, each table took five craftsmen in his shop approximately fifty hours to build, much longer than a modern table.

Finely detailed edges shine on one of the replica tables.

If the workmanship was meticulous, so was the research that preceded it.

Through the years, much of the Capitol's original furniture had been lost, and many of the old items that remained were not original. Thus, state officials, using old documents, photographs and catalogs, spent months determining which tables, chairs, bookcases, benches, library magazine racks and pigeonhole cabinets were authentic.

The Capitol's original wood furniture was purchased from A.H. Andrews & Company, of Chicago, for $50,000. Because of scheduling miscues, it was delivered in early 1889, months after the statehouse opened.

For Joslin and his crew, the project was pride. Standing alongside a finished table in his shop just before it was delivered to the Capitol in 1994, Joslin rubbed its smooth finish and carefully explained its unique features.

"This is doing something for history, something I know my own grandkids will see," Joslin said. ★

A row of photographs record the secretaries of state, an official recordkeeper of Texas, on a wall of the Capitol office. At left is an old seal used to stamp official documents.

Applause swept over Barbara Jordan the first time she walked onto the Senate floor as a Texas legislator. She was a virtual stranger to the majestic surroundings: an ornate chamber where the state's business was conducted with a self-conscious decorum at walnut desks original to the 1888 Capitol, and beneath a decorative ceiling dotted with etched-glass skylights.

On its walls hung paintings of Texas' greatest battles and heroes, men such as Stephen F. Austin and Lyndon Johnson.

"The Texas Capitol didn't mean anything to me growing up," Jordan says. "It was something not accessible to me as a youngster."

Before Jordan took office in 1967, the Senate was not really accessible to her constituents from Houston's predominantly black Fifth Ward either. That is why they came by the hundreds to applaud the first African-American elected to this chamber since 1883.

The Club

Jordan was apprehensive. She looked up to a sea of black faces in the gallery. "Will I disappoint these people? Will I be able to get anything done in a body like this? . . . Will anybody listen to me?"

Her first act was to raise a finger to her lips and hush the crowd. (It was against Senate rules for spectators to applaud.) They quieted immediately.

This woman, whose mere presence revolutionized the exclusive club of mostly white men, was determined to change Senate tradition by following it.

Above: Its Lone Star encircled by live oak and olive branches, a carved version of the State Seal decorates the Senate Chamber podium. ***Facing page:*** Sunlight glints off a painting beside the chamber rostrum of John H. Reagan, the first chairman of the Texas Railroad Commission and former Texas lawmaker.

"I was going to have to break down any prenotions about what to expect from me simply because I didn't look like the rest of them," she recalls. "You've got to show a willingness to be a good ol' boy."

And she did.

By learning the rules of the club and using them to her benefit, by working with the members, by debating them, by bargaining with them in smoke-filled rooms, and even by playing her guitar for them at parties, she won her place.

It was the same thing the good ol' boys did in what they always considered a gentlemen's club.

Betty King is one of the few women to witness this club at work continuously since she began work there in 1949. She recalls the Upper Chamber at that time as an engaging place populated by "real characters, wonderful characters," from humorous East Texas orators to caustic and rough-edged types.

Legendary legislators with colorful nicknames like the "Lion of Lavaca" and the "Bull of the Brazos" held forth. The

Above: *Flanking the main entry door, a photo panel called a composite displays the members of the Senate of 1993. The tradition of composite panels in both houses dates back more than a century.*
Facing page: *Walnut desks for the 31 senators were purchased for the Capitol when it was new, and are still used.*

Left: With its Victorian drapery and polished brass lights having been returned after an absence of many years, the Senate rostrum again reflects a turn-of-the-century elegance. *Above:* A portrait of Stephen F. Austin, the so-called father of Texas, graces the rostrum.

Reflections

The personality of Bob Bullock sometimes has been described like that of the Capitol: Tough, solid, well-worn, sometimes capable of evoking a sentimental appeal to Texans' patriotism.

Now the lieutenant governor, the mercurial politician has spent most of the last thirty-five years at the granite statehouse, a place that affected his life from the moment he first saw it.

That was in 1950.

Bullock wanted to be an architect, just like his father and brother. So he came to Austin to attend the University of Texas, working as a mailroom worker for the Texas Railroad Commission.

His first visit inside the Capitol, he remembers, "just took my breath away." To

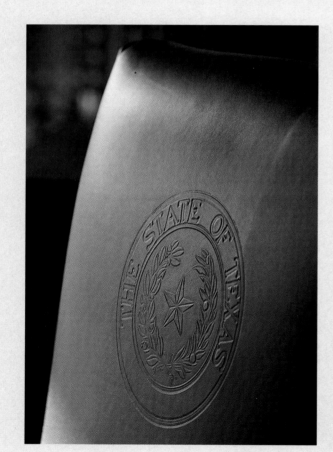

the young man from Hillsboro, the statehouse had a special style: detailed wood and plasterwork, sturdy furniture, an aura of history like no other building he had ever seen. "I couldn't get over the size and its beauty," he said. "The building fascinated me."

Those feelings remain.

After a military stint during the Korean War, Bullock returned in 1957 as a newly elected member of the Texas House, where he served for two years. He had chosen law as his profession, instead of architecture.

As a young lawyer, Bullock argued his first case before the Texas Court of Criminal Appeals in the original third-floor courtroom decorated with ornate woodwork and draperies. He lost the case. "Every time I go by there, I remember that I was so scared," Bullock says.

In 1959, he returned to the Capitol as a lobbyist. Then he stayed on as an assistant attorney general, an aide to Gov. Preston Smith, as secretary of state and as the comptroller of public accounts. In 1991 he was sworn in as lieutenant governor on the Capitol's south steps.

Senators' leather chairbacks in the chamber are branded with the State Seal.

By then, the Capitol was in his blood. Through the years, Bullock said he had tried to visit every corner of the huge building, every niche, from the basement to the top of the dome.

As he explained it, "I always loved Texas history." And the Capitol was at the center of much of it.

"The whole thing is Texas to me," he said. ✯

Left: *"Dawn at the Alamo," a turn-of-the-century depiction of the historic battle in San Antonio, is one of two famous paintings that adorn the rear of the Senate Chamber. The second is "Battle of San Jacinto." Both paintings were done by artist H.A. McArdle.*
Pages 98 and 99: *Beneath a packed gallery, the Senate convenes in January 1995 after a two-year absence. In 1993 the Senate met in temporary quarters in a nearby office building because of the restoration work.*

THE CAPITOL OF TEXAS

Upper Chamber had its own special code of statesmanship where honor, tradition, camaraderie and courtesy were highly regarded.

Despite those high-minded intentions, senators sometimes engaged in name-calling during debates or packed a pistol for protection. It was a place where a group of senators called the Killer Bees stalled state government in 1979, by going into hiding to prove a point, and a place where the thirty-one members knew each other well enough to occasionally take a swing at one another.

The first female senator, Margie Neal of Carthage, joined the club in 1927. By the time King arrived, only the third woman was serving.

In fact, only one woman at a time served in the Senate until 1987, when three were sworn in, nearly seventy years after women won the right to vote in Texas. Four years

Below: *The coffered ceiling in the Senate Chamber is galvanized metal with cast-zinc embellishments and glass-panel skylights. The bowl-like feature at center is one of several original vents designed to circulate air through the large chamber.* **Facing page:** *The original chandeliers radiate light upward onto the decorative ceiling, just above the gallery.*

later, there were four.

For years, most of the top Senate staff members were men. Not until 1951 would the first woman be named as Secretary of the Senate, the top post that King would assume in 1977.

Thirty years after women joined the Senate's ranks, Hispanics followed. In 1957, Henry B. Gonzalez, of San Antonio, became the first state senator of Mexican descent in 110 years.

Ironically, it was primarily Anglos, not Hispanics, who opened the door. "Most Americans of Mexican descent were not able to vote because they had not purchased a poll tax or were not registered to vote," Gonzalez said.

It would be years before the face of Texas politics would change so that minorities and women became an elective force in their own right.

Below an entrance into the Senate Gallery, marked by an etched-glass door transom, an old clock ticks off the legislative hours.

In fact, Gonzalez almost missed his chance to make history. "The filing fee for state Senate was $100 and I had only $5 in my pocket," he says. Gonzalez, a liberal serving on the San Antonio City Council at the time, recalls that several of his colleagues helped raise the filing fee to get him off the council.

Once in the Senate, Gonzalez quickly faced the reality of Texas government in those days.

Seeking to block passage of ten so-called "race bills," or segregation laws, Gonzalez and state Sen. Abraham Kazen Jr., of Laredo carried out what was then the longest filibuster in Senate history, lasting thirty-six hours and two

minutes. In the end, eight of the bills were defeated. The two that passed were later invalidated by the courts.

Later, during a special legislative session in 1957, Gonzalez filibustered for twenty hours in an unsuccesful debate against three segregation bills.

Both times, his simple message echoed through the historic chamber. Even today, the words remain fresh in his mind: "It may be that some can chloroform their conscience. But if we fear long enough, we hate, and if we hate long enough, we fight."

It was not a popular message and Gonzalez often had difficulty being recognized to speak on the Senate floor — until he drafted an unusual ally, Davy Crockett.

"One day I noticed that the (Crockett) statue . . . had become dusty, so I drafted a privileged resolution: 'Whereas through the years the statue of Davy Crockett has become dusty and unclean, be it resolved that it be commissioned to be cleaned'."

The polished brass details of a Senate rostrum light twinkle beneath the chamber's decorative ceiling. The five-arm lights were installed around 1894 and were removed before 1920. The replicas can be removed while the Senate is in session to prevent them from blocking the podium view.

THE CLUB

Reflections

To some people, the forty steep stairs behind the Senate Chamber may seem of little consequence. But to former Lt. Gov. William P. Hobby, the stairs are a lesson in state government.

"If you walk up those steps going from the first floor, in the first flight, there are thirty-two steps — one for each member of the Senate (the senators and the lieutenant governor)," Hobby explains.

The iron railings and tile floors of the Senate back stairs curve gently between floors.

The next flight is shorter, with eight steps representing the governor, attorney general, land commissioner, comptroller, treasurer and three railroad commissioners.

Was this an intentional design touch? Or just a strange coincidence?

In fact, when the Capitol was opened in 1888, the number of steps would not have matched the tally of officialdom. The Railroad Commission was not established until 1891.

Nonetheless, the legend has lived on. In fact, Hobby said he has told the story numerous times.

For Hobby, the Capitol is family.

His grandfather, Edwin M. Hobby, was in the Senate at the time the Legislature voted to build the Capitol, and he later worked there as a commissioner of the Supreme Court. His father, William Pettus Hobby, served as lieutenant governor from 1915 to 1917, and as governor from 1917 to 1921.

The younger Hobby worked there beginning in 1959, as Senate parliamentarian, then as a reporter for *The Houston Post*, and as lieutenant governor from 1973 to 1991, serving in that post longer than any other person.

His favorite spot is the Senate Chamber, where he presided for so many years, a room he describes as "a beautiful space."

"Obviously it has a lot of memories for me, more good, some bad," Hobby says. "But it's just a place I feel very much at home." ★

Such a privileged resolution forced the Senate leadership to let Gonzalez interrupt debate. Once he was recognized, he could then speak on other topics. "This bought me time whenever I needed it to speak my mind (on other topics)!"

Today the Senate is a different place just as Texas is a different place. Yet its best traditions — honor, camaraderie, courtesy and decorum — continue. Gonzalez and Jordan helped effect that.

On the Chamber's walls, alongside artwork depicting the battles of the Alamo and San Jacinto and heroes like Lyndon Johnson and Stephen F. Austin, have been hung the portraits of Jordan and Gonzalez.

Through the use of glass walls, like this one at the end of a hallway leading to the lieutenant governor's office, restoration architects were able to maintain the ambience of the Capitol's original open spaces. The tile floor in the hallway replicates the original.

Above: A copy of the battle flag flown by Texans during the Battle of San Jacinto decorates a wall in the Senate Lounge, a quiet place for members located just behind the chamber. It is not open to the public. *Right:* An eagle and stars decorate a chair in the lounge.

The entrance to the Lieutenant Governor's Reception Room, behind the chamber, features arcing panels of glass decorated with the State Seal.

*J*im Sanders liked the sunny days best. Rays of light glinted through the round, blue windows at the top of the towering atrium rising two stories above the Legislative Reference Library. And the bright hue shimmered into the bookshelves below.

On some days, the sunlight passed through the glass-block floor in the library's center, illuminating a foyer on the level below. If the light was just right, one could stand in the foyer below and watch the shadows of library patrons walking above in a surreal artwork of motion.

Before air conditioning was installed in 1968, the library's tall windows were pushed open on warm days. The birds sang outside and squirrels sometimes scampered onto a ledge for a handout.

"It was really pleasant," says Sanders, who worked in the library from 1959 to 1985, and headed it after 1962.

It was just as its designer intended.

A Beautiful Place

Covering the Capitol's entire north wing on the second floor, the library was the Capitol's largest room other than the legislative chambers. Only it and the Governor's Reception Room, directly across the Rotunda on the second floor, had outside porticoes.

The library was among the most dramatic spaces in the building, thanks to the atrium. It was crowned by a cupola featuring twenty-four round wafers of blue-flashed stained glass, the only colored windows in the building.

The atrium drew much light inside, just like

Above: The brass-handled drawers of the Library's wooden card catalog represent an earlier era. *Facing page:* In one of the Capitol's more spectacular original design touches, atriums stretch upward through two floors, beyond the bookshelves.

THE CAPITOL OF TEXAS

the skylights did in the legislative halls. But the library was more elaborate with its clerestory, a design feature copied from the basilicas of ancient Rome. Colored windows were a bonus.

An awesome sight it was. And for a time, a somewhat vacant one.

The room was built to house a state library that did not exist. The library had burned with the old Capitol in 1881, and was not re-established until three years after the new statehouse opened.

By some accounts, the room was used as a dance hall at the Capitol dedication ceremonies. For two decades thereafter, it housed the state law library in its western half. The State Library was in a room downstairs, part of the Department of Agriculture, Insurance, Statistics and History.

The library did not move into its intended grand home until 1909.

There it remained until 1957, when funds for a new state library and archives building were approved. The law library

Above: From above, the Library's restored floor of glass-block tiles stands out against the patterned carpeting. *Facing page:* Interior lighting and daylight from above in the third-floor atrium cause an artificial rainbow of colors. Arched hallways lead to the Rotunda as the Library lies below.

A BEAUTIFUL PLACE

THE CAPITOL OF TEXAS

Floor-to-ceiling windows and a glass-block floor, in foreground, were designed into the Capitol to increase the natural lighting in the days before electric lights were commonplace. Built for gas lighting, the building was wired for electricity soon after it opened.

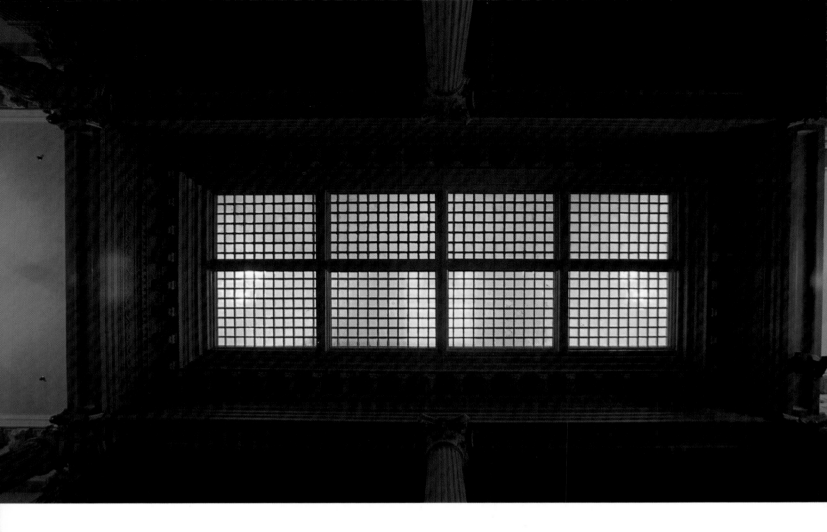

Above: Six of the Library's original eight panels of glass-block tiles were placed in storage after removal in the 1970s and have been reinstalled. This view is from the first-floor lobby. ***Facing page:*** Turn-of-the-century metal bookshelves remain in use, featuring a glass floor on the second tier. Paper hangs from railings for the same reason that earlier librarians hung large photos there: as "modesty panels" to protect women in dresses.

moved out two years later, into the new Supreme Court building. Only the Legislative Reference Library, roughly Texas' equivalent of the Library of Congress, remained in the Capitol room.

When Sally Reynolds began work there in 1966, the original ambiance of the room remained little changed. The double-deck steel bookcases, installed a half-century earlier, were still in use along with oak shelves and tables with green-shaded reading lights. Reynolds, now director of the reference library, remembers the "pretty glass bricks" in the floor, ringed by "yucky brown linoleum."

The room had its problems.

Through the atrium, which employees called "the well," people from the floors above would toss lighted cigarettes, paper wads and spit. Sometimes coins were thrown. "I guess people threw like it was a wishing well," she said. "We were smart enough not to have anything directly under the well."

In 1970, the huge room was subdivided to make space for the Legislative Budget Board. The atrium was closed in and the glass-block floor removed.

Then there were the bats.

Reflections

The view was spectacular, a favorite of the little girl who often stood on tiptoe at the window of her father's Capitol office.

Looking north, from three floors up, Ethel Buckley clearly could see the University of Texas, almost a mile away. Today, though that view was long ago obscured by buildings and trees, her memories remain clear.

As a little girl, Buckley played at the desk of her father, Max Bickler, who served more than forty years in the Capitol as a clerk for the Supreme Court.

Several clerks were housed in a single room of the Capitol's north wing, each one working at an old desk. The tick-tocking of a wall clock was joined by the clatter of manual typewriters. Light bulbs, some hooded with green shades, dangled on wires from the tall ceiling.

On summer days, the large windows were thrown open to entice cool breezes inside.

In those days, through the eyes of a child, the Capitol was a place "where people worked and people from out of town came and went through the Capitol as part of their education."

Buckley remembers the judge who would pass time in a rocking chair in the clerk's office, waiting for an opinion to be filed. "He would sit there and smoke and whittle on the arm of his chair," she says. His initials remain today on the old chair.

Above: Old law books inside one of several glass-fronted shelves.
Facing Page: An iron staircase spirals up one floor from the Library to what once was the chambers of the Supreme Court, now legislative offices.

In many ways, Buckley's family history is inseparable from that of the Capitol. She was born a block north of it, in the Austin Sanitarium. For years her father was the unofficial custodian of the historic, circa-1840 Bible used for a century to swear in Texas governors. When the temporary Capitol burned in 1899, it was a young Max Bickler who sounded the fire alarm.

Years later, after he died, his house yielded Capitol artifacts saved from the trash bin decades before. Among them were some etched-glass transom windows. They were returned to their former places as part of the restoration project. ✭

The west half of the Library once served judges and lawyers. In 1888, when the Capitol opened, the Supreme Court's library boasted 10,000 volumes. Today's state law library has more than 120,000.

Reflections

*Artur Fast worked carefully, measuring the boards time and time
again before he sliced through one with a power saw. Each cut
had to be precise, as the pieces had to fit like a jigsaw puzzle.*

"All the pieces lock together. One goes in first, then another on top of it, then another here," said Fast, pointing to the notches and cuts in a section of wainscoting he was assembling in the Legislative Reference Library.

Fast, a finish carpenter for the Capitol restoration, was duplicating the labors of wood craftsmen a century earlier when they built the Victorian statehouse. He worked with the same precision. And with the like-aged wood.

To replicate and repair the Capitol's millwork, much of it removed or damaged

The ornate oak door pediment is among Capitol woodwork that was painstakingly restored.

since the building had been built, officials had to match it. To do so, they had to track wood that was the same age as the original.

The Capitol's long-leaf yellow pine is an example.

Because of its tight grain, unlike new lumber with less-dense growth rings, only century-old wood would match. That led workers to such unlikely places as an old rock crusher at Knippa, a town west of Uvalde; or a dilapidated warehouse in Port Arthur; or an abandoned cotton compress in Gainesville.

In all, more than nine semi-trailer loads of wood salvaged from those sites and others were used. A twenty-member crew worked for two years to complete the work.

There was a hierarchy to the Capitol's original woods: expensive mahogany in the governor's private office and waiting room, cherry in the Governor's Public Reception Room, walnut in the governor's consultation rooms, red cedar in document rooms, oak in the legislative chambers and hallways and cheaper pine in most other areas.

Restoration of those original woods, in detail that is now not commonly done, was time-consuming and expensive. One doorway required thirty different pieces of molding, each cut separately, in comparison with the three moldings that are used on most modern doorways.

The *Austin Daily Statesman* reported on May 6, 1888, two weeks before the Capitol dedication ceremony:

"The carver and wood-workman who finished up the governor's room at the capitol has purchased all the remnants, and is working them up into beautiful souvenirs, as mementoes of the state capitol."

In 1995, there are no such souvenirs. But the painstaking work by Fast and other workers has restored a much larger keepsake: the Texas Capitol. ⋆

During the summer months, when the library windows were open, migrating bats sometimes clustered in the nooks of the Capitol's craggy exterior. Many times they fluttered in and even roosted in the stacks.

"You would go to get a book and, if you didn't look first, you might grab a bat hanging in there instead," said Brenda Olds, a longtime legislative librarian. "Believe me, we would look before we would reach for a book."

Of all the history tied to the Capitol, the library for many years held the most important. Inside a steel mesh screen attached to the double-deck bookshelves were Texas' most precious archives, including documents from the Alamo and the Civil War.

In addition, many of Texas' laws were researched and written here in the days before the Legislature had its own bill-drafting agency.

Despite its crowding and its peculiarities, the grand room holds many fond memories. Reynolds sums up the sentiment:

"It was one of the few areas in the Capitol you could walk into a room and literally see the whole north wing of the Capitol. It wasn't broken up. You had those big beautiful windows on both sides. And then ... you had those big gorgeous windows in the back.

"It was beautiful."

A library patron studies at a cloth-topped table, one of several that were custom-built to match the originals.

*F*or hours the debate over rural telephones droned on. House leaders, trying to maintain order and a quorum, had locked the doors to the House Chamber and had told members to stay put.

But Pearce Johnson, a legislator representing Travis County, had other ideas: "I wanted to go home, shave ... I was tired of being down there."

So Johnson left, through an open, second-story window on the Capitol's south side.

He inched his way along the narrow stone ledge that girds the statehouse, holding onto the building's rough-edged granite exterior. "That ledge slants a little bit to the outside ... It's not a level ledge," he recalls.

Finally, Johnson found an open window on the west side of the Capitol and stepped inside, much to the surprise of someone who was sitting there.

He said nothing. "I just walked on through and

The People's House

down the stairs out of the Capitol," he recalls.

The story from the late 1940s is just another example of the colorful House at its best. Throughout its history, the lower chamber has been a place of sometimes rambunctious endeavor, where such extremes as fistfights and velvet-tongued diplomacy have guided Texas for more than a century — all beneath architecture that many swear encourages a special statesmanship in the Capitol's largest room.

It is a chamber with personality, where Red

Above: The historic flag carried in the 1836 Battle of San Jacinto, a victory in the Texas War for Independence, is a centerpiece of the House rostrum. The dark patches in the background are remnants of the original fabric. *Facing page:* A view of the rostrum. *Pages 124 and 125:* In January 1995, the House convened in its newly restored chamber with the floor and galleries packed.

Square and Constitution Square were locations on the floor, referring to the political leanings of members whose desks were located there. It is a chamber where demeanor sometimes has been measured by the color of carpet — "fuddy-duddy" gold during the '60s, "energized" bright gold in the '70s, the "busy" blue pattern of the 1980s. And it is a place where tarpaulins once were suspended on ropes below the skylights to keep the heat down and tempers cool.

It also is the chamber that, in 1971, commended the Boston Strangler for his efforts at population control and, two years later, voted to require felons to give twenty-four hours' notice before they committed a crime. It was from the House gallery the same year that the Apache Belles, a Tyler drill team, suggested that lawmakers get serious about an ethics bill: They turned bottoms up to spell out "r-e-f-o-r-m."

The image at top shows a portrait of Sam Houston in an ornate frame hanging near the voting board, which lists legislators' names in columns: ALONZO, ALVARADO, AVERITT, BAILEY, BERLANGA, BLACK, BOMER, BOSSE, BRADY, BRIMER, CARONA, CARTER, CHISUM, CLEMONS, COLEMAN, COMBS, CONLEY, COOK, CORTE, COUNTS, CRABB, CRADDICK, CUELLAR H., CUELLAR R., CULBERSON, DANBURG, DAVILA, DAVIS; DEAR, DELISI, DENNY, DRIVER, DUKES, DUNCAN, DUTTON, EDWARDS, EHRHARDT, EILAND, ELKINS, FARRAR, FINNELL, GALLEGO, GIDDINGS, GLAZE, GOODMAN, GUTIERREZ, HAGGERTY, HAMRIC, HARRIS, HARTNETT, HAWLEY, HEFLIN, HERNANDEZ, HIGHTOWER; HILBERT, HILDERBRAN, HILL, HIRSCHI, HOCHBERG, HOLZHEAUSER, HORN, HOWARD, HUDSON, HUNTER B., HUNTER T., JACKSON, JANEK, JOHNSON, JONES D., JONES, LEWIS JR., LONGORIA, LUNA, MADDEN, MARCHANT, MAXEY, McCALL, McCLENDON.

Above: A portrait of Sam Houston, near the voting board, has hung in the House Chamber since 1907.
*Below: Members vote electronically by punching buttons on a brass keypad on the desk. **Facing page:** The image of the wooden window shutters in the Chamber is reflected in the glass on one of the composite panels hanging nearby.*

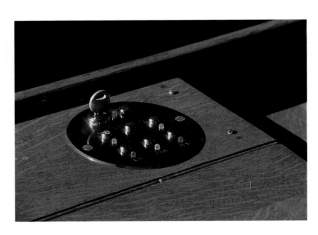

Amid such occasional tomfoolery even came gunplay.

Former state legislator Chet Brooks, who first came to work at the Capitol in 1954 as a cub reporter, remembers the story of a Houston representative who kept a six-gun in his desk on the House floor — "a long barrel ... like an old .45, something out of a western movie.

"If he'd get excited in arguing, he'd reach in his desk and pull that gun out and wave it around," said Brooks.

"He never shot anybody ... Of course, the speaker and everybody would just get terribly upset ... and try to get him to put that gun away or take it away from him or something."

If a House member's small oak desk on the chamber floor occasionally doubled as gun storage, it also was the legislator's only office for years. Elected to the House in 1963, Brooks recalls that he stored all

HOUSE OF REPRESENTATIVES

SEVENTY-FIRST LEGISLATURE

Reflections

Texans have special feelings for their Capitol, a certain reverence or awe. The place holds a special kinship with Jean Houston Daniel, former First Lady of Texas, mother of a House speaker, descendant of legendary Texas hero Sam Houston.

The old granite statehouse and her family, she explains, have played roles in each other's lives since the day the Capitol was dedicated in 1888.

It was then that Temple Houston, who was the son of Sam Houston and was Daniel's great-great-uncle, gave the dedicatory speech. A well-known orator, plainsman and lawyer, he called the Capitol "the noblest edifice upon this hemisphere…Here glitters a structure that shall stand as a sentinel of eternity."

Nearly a half-century later, in 1937, Jean Daniel worked inside that noblest edifice, part-time for the Secretary of the Senate while she was a student at the University of Texas at Austin. She returned six years later as the wife of Price Daniel, the House speaker. The Capitol became home for them and their two young children in the speaker's quarters behind the House Chamber.

"At that time, the apartment had only one bedroom and secretaries and typewriters were in an adjoining hallway. There was no back elevator and I had to choose between climbing up and down the long back stairs or going through the House Chamber with children and groceries," she said.

Jean Houston Daniel, with the Capitol dome behind her.

"Regardless, this was one of the happiest and most challenging times in our forty-eight years of marriage."

Price Daniel would later serve as attorney general, as U.S. senator, as governor and as a Texas Supreme Court justice. A son, Price Daniel Jr., would serve as House speaker in 1973, thirty years after his father.

"Most Texans think a great deal of the Capitol," she says. "I have a lot of pride in it." ✮

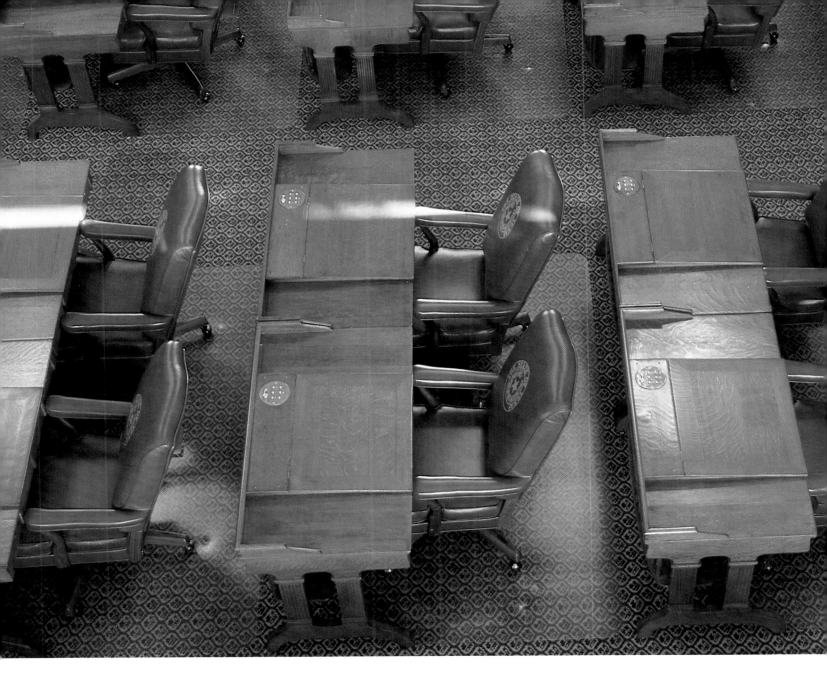

his work papers in a Cutty Sark box beneath his desk. Only top House leaders enjoyed the luxury of private offices.

When the 1888 Capitol first opened, there were no desks. Because of a delay in ordering new furniture, the first Legislature to meet in the new Capitol worked for several weeks on old chairs and tables. And even after the desks and chairs arrived in February 1889, two months after lawmakers convened, the speaker's private office and seven House committee rooms were among the thirty-seven rooms and nine halls left unfurnished for lack of money.

For years, members relied on a pool of secretaries who worked at typewriters lining the back hallway outside the House speaker's office or in a large room just downstairs

Bathed in a soft glow of light from the brass chandeliers overhead, legislators' desks in the House Chamber shine.

Reflections

Ornately star-shaped, each spelling out T-E-X-A-S in lightbulbs or brass, the polished chandeliers in each legislative chamber were specially selected.

Like sparkling crowns beneath the ornate ceiling and etched-glass skylights, the large luminaires survived — while most other original Capitol light fixtures were replaced through the years.

The fixtures are among the Capitol's signature decorations, like the colorful Rotunda floor or the Goddess of Liberty atop the dome, and they have on occasion provided inspiration as well as light.

For example, during a debate in 1977, state Rep. Irma Rangel of Kingsville, newly elected and the first Mexican-American woman to serve in the House, pushed to provide more money for indigent women and their children. But amid the usual din of House proceedings, few colleagues were listening.

Then, bang. A lightbulb exploded in one of the chandeliers. The chamber fell silent.

"I told them, 'Hey, someone up there is trying to send a message to you guys … Support this amendment,'" Rangel recalls. "It passed. Other amendments on that program had failed before. But this time it passed."

For Rangel, it was a proud moment. Growing up in South Texas, the Capitol had never much been part of her world, nor that of much of Texas' Mexican-American population. She and her parents had never even visited the statehouse until she was sworn in.

Now, her voice had made a difference, even with a little help from a chandelier that said "Texas." ✯

Right: *One of the Chamber's chandeliers that spells T-e-x-a-s.*
Facing page: *The open shutters bathe the Chamber in sunlight Natural light is one of the most important qualities that was restored with the building, officials say.*

THE CAPITOL OF TEXAS

The glow from hallway lights illuminates the etched-glass transom that has marked the entry into the House Gallery for a century.

from the chamber. Switchboard operators rang members' calls through to a long line of phone booths in the hallway behind the chamber.

In the 1960s, when state agencies began moving out of the Capitol, enough space became available for all House members finally to have individual offices. But two members had to share each tiny office, most of which were little bigger than a closet.

Brooks recalls that when constituents came to see his office mate, "I'd get up and go outside so they could all get in there and talk to him. When people came to see me, he'd do the same thing."

When House Speaker Pete Laney arrived, in January 1973 as a freshman representative, he picked an

Above: Rows of wooden-backed seats in the Gallery, shined and ready for the next group of constituents who come to see the laws being made. *Below:* The mirrored doors of a Victorian cabinet in the House Members' Lounge provide a double image of a wall clock nearby.

Reflections

For years, the old photograph was little more than a family memento. Taken in 1905, it showed Samuel Ealy Johnson Jr., a turn-of-the-century lawmaker and the father of President Lyndon Johnson, sitting in a swivel chair in the House Chamber.

Then it was discovered by a State Preservation Board researcher, searching for clues on what the original carpeting in the House chamber looked like.

State files that contained those details had been lost years ago. But the black-and-white photo provided a clue, even though the detail was hazy.

What came next was an historical detective project that led Darlene Marwitz, a Preservation Board historian, to various sources across the United States. The result is the colorful carpeting in the House, a replica of what was there years ago, when Sam Johnson served.

From an enlargement of the photo, Marwitz carefully measured the spread of the legs on the swivel chair. She knew the measurements of the chair and used them to determine the size of the carpet pattern. She then drew the pattern on tracing paper.

Then, the search began to track down more details of the design, including the colors. Files in the Smithsonian Institution in Washington were researched. Antique-carpet experts, even the archives of a longtime carpet manufacturer, were consulted. Marwitz even tracked some leads while on a family vacation.

Finally, after extensive research, she verified the likely color and pattern. Once tufts of colored yarn were closely compared to find the right color, the special carpet for the House Chamber was made in England.

A divider rail's brass base, reflecting a distorted view of the Chamber, is surrounded by the distinctive pattern of the replica carpeting.

The original probably was made in England as well, officials said, in strips approximately two feet wide that were hand-sewn together. Likewise, the replicated carpeting was brought from England by boat and sewn together at the Capitol by installers.

In all, officials said, the restoration of original-looking carpeting proved probably the most involved aspect of refurnishing the statehouse in its correct style.

Seven original carpets have been replicated, from an unusual blue-swirl pattern in the Governor's original office to a floral design in the Supreme Court Room. There, the research was simpler because a small piece of the original, removed in the 1930s, had inadvertantly been preserved in an Austin museum.

For Marwitz, the tedious work paid off.

By restoring several Capitol rooms to their original designs, state officials hoped Texans could better experience their history. The carpeting, she said, "is as much a part of the architecture as it is the style of the building."

Surely, Sam Johnson might appreciate that. ✫

office on the fourth floor in the south wing, one with a majestic view down Congress Avenue.

Years earlier he had seen it through a child's eyes when he had visited the Capitol with his grandfather, had climbed to the top of the dome and had stood in awe of the Capitol's magnificence.

"You saw things in there that were only in one place ... paintings and statues, all original things ... Everybody we ran into made you feel like it was your building," he recalls. "The people didn't awe me as much as the building."

In the halls, he studied the large framed photographs of House members, one for each Legislature dating back to 1866.

A gavel stands at the ready in the Speaker's Office, behind the House Chamber. A single-arm brass light accents the shiny woodwork and etched-glass panels in the door.

Now, Laney's picture is up there among all those others who have served in the so-called House of the People. The chamber is a place where governors have been inaugurated, and where a cross section of the world has come to speak to Texas — from presidents and astronauts to the Queen of England and country-western singers.

It is also a place for Texans such as Laney, a cotton farmer from tiny Hale Center in West Texas.

All are a part of history that, to some, is as awe-inspiring as the building itself.

"It puts your job in perspective," Laney said. "The magnificence of the building makes you realize that you're dealing with lots of things ... You realize that what you're doing affects a lot of people's lives.

Above: Sunlight illuminates the glass panels in the House Chamber ceiling, as one of the brass chandeliers hangs beneath it.
Facing page: Viewed from below, the coffered ceiling of the chamber is like a colorful checkerboard, with the chandelier as a gamepiece.

"You look around and sometimes it scares you. You think, how did you get there? ... I'm just a guy from West Texas ... It's more that you hope what you're doing, or what the body's doing, is right. I think that all the individuals in the gallery and the massiveness of the room puts you in that mood of hoping."

SICUT PATRIBUS, SIT DEUS NOBIS

*Th*ey came to the court with pistols on their hips, but they were not wearing badges. As one might expect in Texas, the issues were oil and money.

On this day, during the 1920s, the imposing Supreme Court Room on the Texas Capitol's third floor was packed with ranchers who had at stake millions of dollars in royalties, the money paid to them for the oil beneath their land.

The mood was as somber as the surroundings — high ceilings, a drapery-bedecked bench bearing a Latin phrase, formally dressed lawyers sitting at the long and curving tables topped with green billiard cloth. Or so the story goes.

"The day that (case) was argued the room was just full of West Texas people. Most of them had a pistol on their hips. I don't think they made them take them off," recalls Joe R. Greenhill, a former chief justice who heard the tale as a young law student during the late 1930s.

Years have blurred the details of that tense

Halls of Justice

episode. But as far as anyone remembers, no shots were fired. And eventually, the landowners got to keep their royalties — but not before some legal setbacks that enraged Texans and, as Greenhill remembers, left the Legislature believing "they had a communist Supreme Court."

Those were the kind of dramas played out in the historic courtroom, a place that for years was looked to as the world authority on oil and gas law when Texas was the Oil King.

It was also a room where sat the only all-woman Supreme Court ever convened in the

Above: Senate Journals from 1889, the year after the Capitol opened, contain laws which the Supreme Court has reviewed. *Facing page:* A rich canopy of gold drapery and paintings of justices tower over the Supreme Court Room bench, decorated with the Latin phrase: "As God was to our forefathers, so may he be to us."

Behind a star-backed chair, a Capitol original, paintings of former judges line a wall in the Supreme Court Room.

United States. Gov. Pat Neff named three women, in 1925, to decide a case involving a fraternal organization to which all three sitting male justices belonged.

Through the Capitol courtrooms passed a case where, during the 1940s, a young lawyer named Thurgood Marshall argued to admit African-Americans to the University of Texas School of Law. His arguments would be affirmed by the U.S. Supreme Court, on which Marshall later would serve as that court's first black justice.

For years, the three justices on the Texas Supreme Court were so busy that six appointed lawyers, called commissioners, worked alongside them, researching and hearing cases. In 1945, the court was expanded to nine justices, all working in space built for three.

Greenhill, an Austin lawyer, first came to the Capitol in 1932, as a college freshman; he worked as an unpaid mailroom worker for his mother, who was the state's first child welfare chief.

In 1940, Greenhill was hired as a Supreme Court law clerk, working in a makeshift room formed by bookcases in a Capitol hallway. It was there, the day after Pearl Harbor

Left: The only all-woman Supreme Court ever appointed in the nation was named in 1925 to hear a case involving the fraternal organization Woodmen of the World, of which all three male justices were members. Left to right, Associate Justice Hattie Henenberg, Chief Justice Hortense Ward and Associate Justice Ruth Brazzil, were selected by Gov. Pat Neff to decide the case. All three were lawyers.

Pages 144 and 145: *The restored Supreme Court Room looks much as it did when the Capitol was new, down to the curved tables for lawyers and brass light fixtures. Carpet was replicated using a piece of the original that was saved years ago and preserved in a museum. The high court had three members when the Capitol was new.*

Reflections

Ralph Yarborough's first Capitol office was not fancy, "a pigeon-hole-like thing" with an old desk flanked by several filing cabinets. In the summertime, fans circulated the stale air back and forth through open windows.

But it was here, in 1931, that Yarborough's long and distinguished political career began. He was one of seventeen assistants to then-Attorney General Jimmy Allred, who later would become governor.

The office was on the first floor, on the south side of the Capitol's west wing, where the attorney general's office was located until it was moved into a nearby office building about 1960.

As a young lawyer who had been reared in the cotton patches and cornfields of East Texas, Yarborough drew inspiration from the old building and from the people who served there.

It was in an office adjacent to Yarborough's where James Stephen Hogg, an idol of Yarborough, once served. The legendary Hogg, who later became governor, was attorney general when the Capitol was completed in 1888.

From the gallery in the House Chamber, Yarborough watched as Miriam "Ma" Ferguson was sworn into office in 1933, with the shortest inauguration speech ever:

"Roses are red and violets are blue.
If you love me like I love you,
No knife can cut our love in two."

Yarborough looks back on that speech as the most memorable event he ever witnessed at the Texas Capitol. "Didn't sound like a governor of Texas to me. Unlike anything I ever envisioned," he says.

Once, while Yarborough was an assistant attorney general, he negotiated a lawsuit settlement with an oil company, the second largest recovery in state history. He proudly presented Allred with a million-dollar check.

Star design on chairback was a feature of Capitol originals.

But his boss balked. "He said, 'Let's see that' and acted like he was mad," Yarborough said. Allred then called the oil company lawyers in and "cussed them out and everything so they raised it $73,500 more."

Afterward, he remembers, "Jimmy would go around ... and say, 'Well, Ralph got the million dollars but, by God, I got that $73,500.'" ✭

in December, 1941, that he and members of the Supreme Court clustered around a small radio to hear President Roosevelt declare war on Japan.

In 1947, he became an assistant attorney general and joined the high court in 1957. Through those years, he recalls the Capitol as "just a granite barn," an uncomfortable place to work — "hot as hell in the summer and cold as hell in the winter."

The heat was among the reasons Texas justices did not wear the traditional black robes until the 1960s, when they moved into air-conditioned quarters outside the Capitol.

The justices' chambers were furnished with the only beds bought for the new Capitol, so-called Murphy beds, the fold-up type. In those days, the court met in Austin, Tyler

Court business paused briefly in 1900 for this photo. Members of the court pictured are Chief Justice Reuben R. Gaines, and Associate Justices T.J. Brown and F.A. Williams. Court Clerk Charles S. Morse and Deputy Clerk Fred T. Connerly stand to the left of the bench. Note the bare light bulb hanging between door and column.

and Galveston and some justices roomed in the Capitol.

Though the hot Capitol could be uninviting, it was inspiring.

As a law student, another former chief justice, Robert W. Calvert, often watched hearings in the Capitol courtroom. It was there that the orphan from Corsicana, who began work at the Capitol in 1923 as an elevator operator, first began to realize his ambitions, leading to a public service career spanning fifty years.

He served as House speaker in 1937, a Supreme Court justice from 1950 to 1972 and a chairman of the Texas Constitutional Revision Commission in 1976. He died in 1994 at age eighty-nine.

From his days as a Capitol elevator operator, Calvert recalled that his ambitions were as grand as the building. "I was going to make it somewhere. I wasn't going to be a throw-away or anything of that sort."

When Jack Hightower joined the Texas House, just two years out of law school in 1953, the native of tiny Memphis, Texas, in the Panhandle, drew inspiration from the courtroom. It was there that he watched Dan Moody — former governor, constitutional scholar, highly regarded lawyer. "What am I doing here?" Hightower, a justice since 1987, remembers thinking.

It was Hightower who, as a state senator from 1966 to 1974, oversaw major renovations in the east wing to accommodate additional offices for senators. His orders: Make everything look as original as possible, from plaster walls to oak wainscoting.

In contrast, he recalls, remodeling of the House side took a different tack. "They ripped out that beautiful wainscoting, put up this cheap, cheap-looking plywood paneling ... It would just make me sick to go down there and see what they were doing," Hightower recalls.

After the court vacated its Capitol quarters in 1960 to move into a new building nearby, lawmakers left the courtroom relatively intact for legislative hearings. Only the Court of Appeals courtroom, located across the hall from the Supreme Court, underwent partial subdividing into legislative offices.

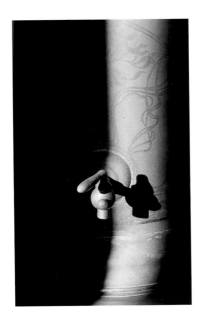

Above: A stripe of sunlight reveals painted detail on an old water cooler in the restored Supreme Court Room. *Facing page:* Replicated from old photos, the swivel chairs of the justices stand in line behind the bench.

Reflections

*Archie Sweazea slowly pulled the wet brush across the soft plaster,
smoothing out several tiny bumps in the intricate design.
He paused and studied his progress.*

Then, after a few more swipes with the paintbrush, he smiled.

"It's not difficult, once you learn how to do it," he said.

A few minutes earlier, the wet plaster had been only a gooey white blob in a plastic pail. Now it was part of an ornate cornice, decorating the ceiling in the original courtroom of the Court of Appeals on the Texas Capitol's third floor.

If Sweazea were a painter, the walls and ceilings of the statehouse would be his canvas. For most of his adult life, he has been a plasterer, an artisan in white mud. A commonplace trade when the statehouse was opened in 1888, it is one few people now practice.

The decorative plasterwork is a key feature of the restored Capitol, from the rosettes and swirls that run along the walls to the square shapes and cast-in-place moldings that ring the high ceilings in most rooms. While wall plastering is still commonly done, decorative plastering with the Capitol's degree of detail is not.

Delicate rosettes in Capitol plaster trimwork were cast by hand, originally and during the restoration.

Work involved molding the wet plaster into the elaborate designs on the Capitol's walls and ceilings, much of which had been torn out years ago or damaged by earlier remodeling. Workers used tools with names like "mule" and "hawk," and knew the difference between architectural details like cornice and dentil.

First the crew made rubber molds of every plaster detail to be replicated — "twenty coats of rubber, two a day," according to Sweazea. From those molds, many details were precast from wet plaster. Once dry, they were then carefully glued onto the walls and ceilings with wet plaster.

Much of the detail, however, was cast in place from more wet plaster. To do that, crew members cut tin forms, called "mules," of the profiles of the trim. They troweled wet plaster onto the wall and pulled the mule through it to form the design.

It was a tedious process. Sometimes the plasterers had to repeat the step again and again until the wet plaster was formed just right.

In restoring history, the plasterers repeated it. Explains Sweazea:

"We're doing it basically the same way crews would have done it when they built the Capitol ... Plastering is the oldest trade, I think, even older than carpentry. I think Noah was a plasterer." ★

Now the two courtrooms have been returned to their original glory, for a new life as places for legislation rather than justice. Lawmakers also will occupy the nearby offices where judges once toiled in the summer heat.

It is fitting, says Hightower, president of the Texas Supreme Court Historical Society. After all, the laws made and interpreted in those rooms play a major role in the lives of Texans, just as those gun-toting West Texas ranchers once made so clear.

Home to the Supreme Court for nearly half its existence, "this room ... saw the court develop the law of the state from the time when we were ... recovering from the effects of a lost war to the development of the great railroad industry criss-crossing the state to the discovery of oil and gas," said Supreme Court Chief Justice Tom Phillips during an October 1994 rededication ceremony.

Standing on the sun-bleached stone steps of the old General Land Office, Garry Mauro looks toward the Capitol dome rising above the tall oaks and elms. He feels goose bumps on his arms.

"Can you imagine?" he says. "It took a lot of guts to build that kind of Capitol like that in Austin, Texas, thinking we would ever need one that big."

It was vision with a capital V, a sense of thinking big and accomplishing that goal in one of the most unique land swaps ever. The deal brought what was touted at the time as the world's seventh-largest building to a town of less than 15,000 people. And it gave a cash-strapped state a multimillion-dollar showplace.

As Texas land commissioner, Mauro has a unique perspective on the feat. Inside the tan, stucco land office, his predecessors oversaw the deals that built the Capitol, brought in railroads and industry and financed public education.

Legacy of Land

All that was done with Texas' public lands, the state's biggest source of wealth. Dirt was like gold. Control of that wealth lay within the land office, a place where surveys were filed and where draftsmen penned the maps. It was, literally, the bank for Texas riches — and the depository of some of the state's oldest documents, including Spanish land grants from the 1700s.

Originally housed in log cabins, the land office, by 1851, was in a small building located where the west wing of the Capitol now stands.

Above: A star-shaped transom design is a distinctive feature of the Land Office building. *Facing page:* Like a jewel box in a forest of emerald-green trees that surround the Capitol, the 1857 Land Office is the oldest state office building, thirty-one years older than its domed neighbor.

Designed by an architect who once served a Russian czar, the Land Office's highly formal design symmetry and round-arched windows are considered Medieval in character. It was built for $50,698, and is considered one of the most historically significant buildings in Texas.

Those quarters quickly proved too small.

Then, thanks to a land deal that would be a prelude to one that would finance the Capitol nearly four decades later, a new land office was erected. The Medieval castle has become an Austin landmark at the southeast edge of the Capitol grounds.

Gov. Elisha M. Pease is credited with carrying out that vision.

At a time when most of state government was housed in log or wood-frame buildings, Pease wanted the new state to have fine examples of several architectural styles. As part of the Compromise of 1850, Texas received $10 million for relinquishing its claim to Eastern New Mexico. It used about half the money to build eight state buildings, including the 1857 land office at the southeast edge of Capitol Hill.

Replaced in 1917, the land office building gradually deteriorated into a shabby and decaying relic. By 1989, one official suggested it should be bulldozed.

But now, thanks to a $3.1 million restoration timed to coincide with the renovation of the 1888 Capitol, the state's oldest government office building has been rejuvenated to house a visitor's center and a history gallery.

Though long overshadowed by the Capitol in prestige and attention, the land office is just as rich in history.

It was one of the first state buildings designed by a trained architect, Christoph Conrad Stremme, a German-born designer who worked for a Russian czar before coming to Texas in 1849. He also worked as a draftsman in the land office.

Noted Texas artist Hermann Lungkwitz also worked there, as did Martha Lungkwitz, a patent clerk and probably the state's first full-time female employee, in 1872.

The building was home to one of Texas' first photographic darkrooms, which was used to reproduce land maps.

And it was the place where William Sydney Porter, author of enduring short stories under the pen name O. Henry, worked as a draftsman from 1887 to 1891. Porter used the building as a setting for two stories, referring to it in one: "You think of the Rhine; the 'castled crag of Drachenfels' ... and the vine-clad slopes of Germany."

The land office building was one of the most extensively planned state buildings prior to the Civil War. Stremme prepared twenty-two drawings, compared to only five drawn for the 1856 Governor's Mansion and only two for the circa 1852 Capitol.

Special design touches are evident throughout the building. The limestone steps on its spiral staircase were cut by hand so as to fit together perfectly. Window frames were designed to shed water and seal themselves, years before the advent of weatherstripping. The downspouts were recessed into the exterior walls to prevent detraction from the architecture. The front door was built into an alcove to help cool the interior, decades before

A parapet wall above the windows shows Norman style. Stucco exterior is scored to make it look as if the building is built from cut stone.

THE CAPITOL OF TEXAS

An iron staircase winds between floors below arched windows, each with interior wooden shutters. Though most had been removed years before, the star-shaped windows were replicated during the restoration project.

Right: From the first floor, near the vault where Spanish land grants once were housed, the main staircase ascends from a lobby. *Pages 160 and 161:* Spiraling like a sea shell, the stone stairway that stretches from the attic to the first floor has interlocking steps. Short story writer O. Henry, who worked as a draftsman in the building, used it in one of his famous tales. He once wrote that the Land Office "has been consecrated by the touch of hands that Texas will never cease to honor."

THE CAPITOL OF TEXAS

Reflections

*In a hallway just north of the Capitol Rotunda, Wallace Ellis
and Emily May Carter first met when the twentieth century
was only five years old.*

It was love at first sight for May, a Uvalde schoolteacher in her early twenties, and Wallace, an employee of the Railroad Commission who was nineteen years her senior.

They married. Numerous times after Wallace was killed by a drunken driver in 1923 while they were enjoying a Sunday drive, May would return to the spot where they met.

"She was so sentimental about that spot," their daughter, Virginia Ellis Adcock of Austin, explained. "She just loved the Capitol."

May, who died in 1967, never remarried.

Today that love is memorialized at the Esplanade at the north entrance to the Capitol, above the Capitol Extension, as part of the commemorative paver project. There a walkway paved with twelve-by-twelve-inch granite stones preserves memories.

The project was launched in 1987 as a fund-raising tool for the Capitol restoration. In all, 2,183 pavers were sold for $300 apiece. The Adcocks bought their paver in 1993 to honor her parents and to celebrate their own fifty-fifth wedding anniversary.

For many, perhaps, these pavers are a stone version of vanity license plates, a place where politicians can record their place in history and where families can honor their ancestors or observe anniversaries. Fittingly, it is a place where folks can brag about being Texans.

The Ellis' paver, atop the Capitol Extension.

The sunset-pink stones record an eclectic cross-section of Texas: elementary school classes; law firms and judges; noted pianist Van Cliburn; cowboy star Gene Autry; Big Oil; a fast-food business; sons of Confederate veterans; bikers and bowlers; ranchers; Dallas' Adolphus Hotel — all cemented side by side. One person bought a stone to honor President Reagan. A Houston man bought thirty-three, to honor his relatives. All but seventeen of Texas' 254 counties bought them, as did dozens of cities and towns.

Behind each is a story. One can walk along and imagine: "Port Aransas. Living on Island Time." "Joe Lockett Rosson. A true son of Texas." "Lou H. Froh, a wonderful Texan." "Rose F. Parsley, proud native Texan."

If the Capitol restoration was a product of love, then surely so were many of the pavers. Love like Wallace and May Ellis had for each other, a love now carved in stone. ✯

air-conditioning.

The building's stucco exterior was crafted to make it appear like cut stone. And on each end was a Lone Star, the remnant of a grander design Stremme had planned. He wanted an array of fancy exterior ornaments surrounding the stars: oxen, horse heads and plows.

For Mauro, the restoration of the old castle is a fitting tribute to the vision of his predecessors.

In the drafting room, land maps were prepared that documented Texas' holdings. A surreal scene has been created with historic furniture and cutouts from a circa-1890 photo of Land Office workers.

Reflections

*When Wilhelmina Delco first came to the Texas Capitol in 1975
as a newly elected state representative from Austin, she quickly
realized its grand architecture was only part of its symbolism.*

From the Capitol's steps, Delco could see the historic cultural diversity that is Texas, perhaps as nowhere else. Truly, she believes that the statehouse is a crossroads of Texas.

If one looks to the north of the Capitol, she says, there is the University of Texas with its sprawling campus, "the largest flagship university and one of the wealthiest university centers of learning in the country." Beyond it are middle-class neighborhoods of Austin.

To the east are working-class and poor neighborhoods. "You're looking toward Huston-Tillotson, one of the oldest historically black institutions in the country, which is firmly anchored ... in a community that is struggling to survive, not just to grow," she explains.

To the south, through the Capitol's main door, where generations of Texans have arrived at the statehouse "with such great hope and expectation," is Austin's central business district, expensive real estate dotted with tall buildings. And beyond that, across the Lower Colorado River, are neighborhoods where "a large part of the Mexican-American community settled."

*Below: View from
the Capitol dome
looking toward the
University of Texas.
Facing page: A
Lone Star visage,
the Capitol dome
as seen through
one of the Land
Office's star-
shaped windows.*

To the west, at the edge of the rolling Hill Country of Texas, "is Enfield, where some of the richest, most powerful people in Texas live."

"Out of any given window, you're looking at significant chunks, not just of history, but significant population differences that have a tremendous interest in what we're doing in that building," says Delco, who in 1991 became the first African-American woman to serve as speaker pro-tem.

"Whether you come up the east, west, north or south walk, you're coming to a forum where hopefully you'll meet ...To be able to see to the Capitol from all those vantage points, to be able to come to the Capitol from all those vantage points and (to)...feel all those aspects of Austin, Texas, from that Capitol, is just as important." ✶

THE CAPITOL OF TEXAS

THE CAPITOL

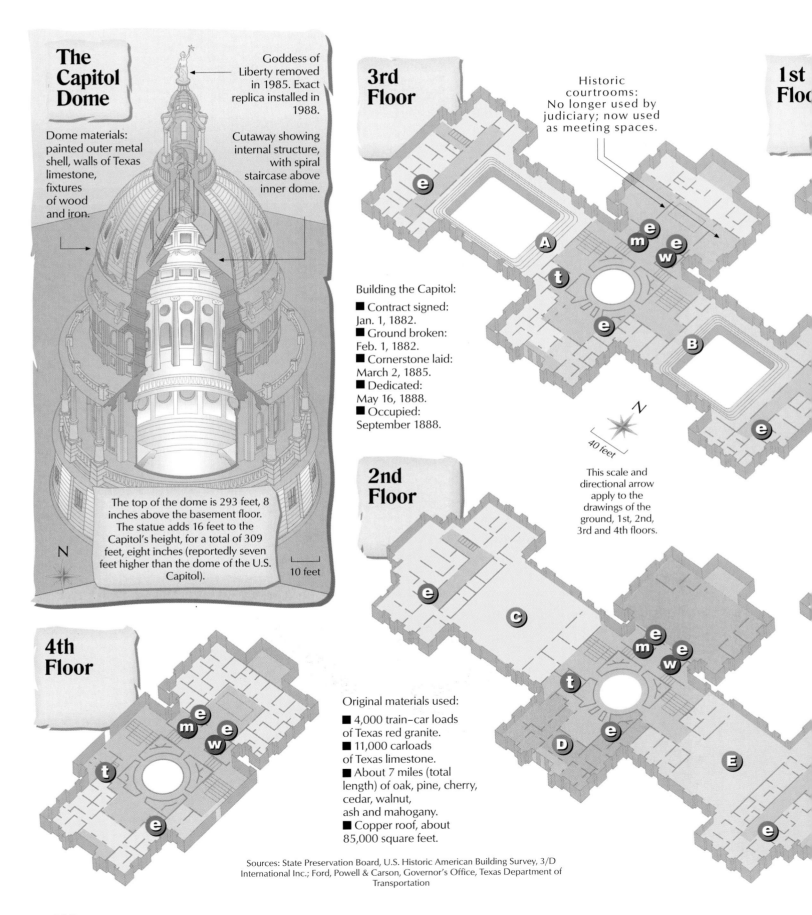

The Capitol Dome

Dome materials: painted outer metal shell, walls of Texas limestone, fixtures of wood and iron.

Goddess of Liberty removed in 1985. Exact replica installed in 1988.

Cutaway showing internal structure, with spiral staircase above inner dome.

The top of the dome is 293 feet, 8 inches above the basement floor. The statue adds 16 feet to the Capitol's height, for a total of 309 feet, eight inches (reportedly seven feet higher than the dome of the U.S. Capitol).

N

10 feet

3rd Floor

Historic courtrooms: No longer used by judiciary; now used as meeting spaces.

1st Floor

Building the Capitol:
- Contract signed: Jan. 1, 1882.
- Ground broken: Feb. 1, 1882.
- Cornerstone laid: March 2, 1885.
- Dedicated: May 16, 1888.
- Occupied: September 1888.

N

40 feet

This scale and directional arrow apply to the drawings of the ground, 1st, 2nd, 3rd and 4th floors.

2nd Floor

4th Floor

Original materials used:
- 4,000 train-car loads of Texas red granite.
- 11,000 carloads of Texas limestone.
- About 7 miles (total length) of oak, pine, cherry, cedar, walnut, ash and mahogany.
- Copper roof, about 85,000 square feet.

Sources: State Preservation Board, U.S. Historic American Building Survey, 3/D International Inc.; Ford, Powell & Carson, Governor's Office, Texas Department of Transportation

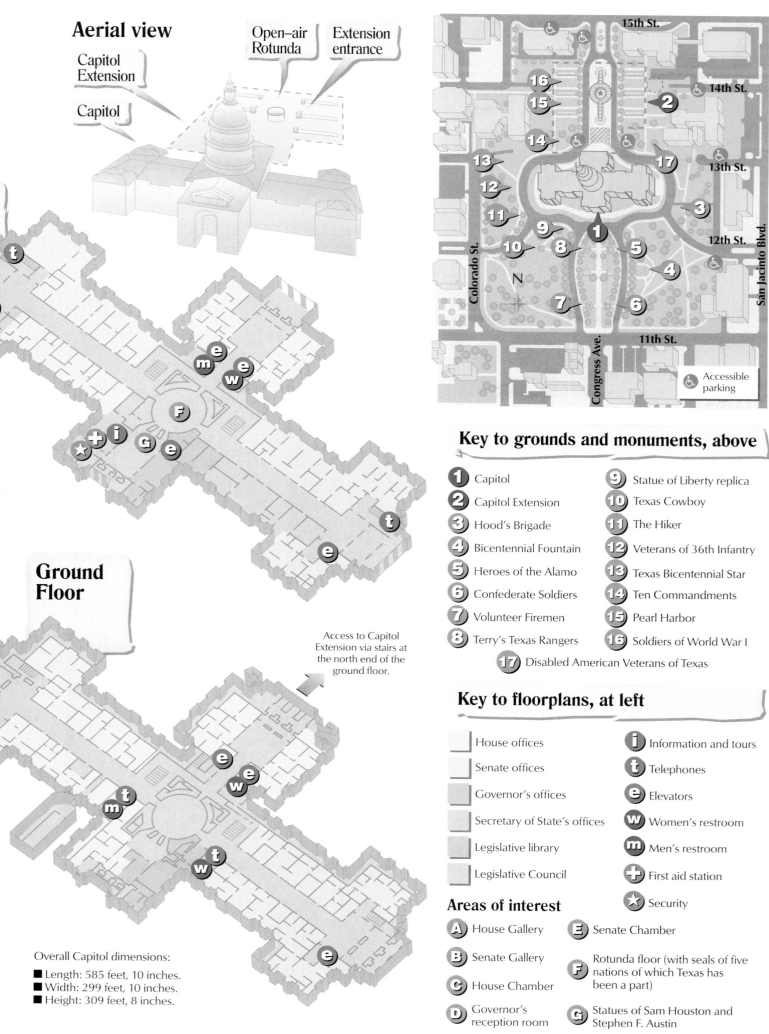

Aerial view

Capitol Extension

Open–air Rotunda

Extension entrance

Capitol

Capitol

Ground Floor

Access to Capitol Extension via stairs at the north end of the ground floor.

Overall Capitol dimensions:
- Length: 585 feet, 10 inches.
- Width: 299 feet, 10 inches.
- Height: 309 feet, 8 inches.

15th St.

14th St.

13th St.

12th St.

11th St.

Colorado St.

San Jacinto Blvd.

Congress Ave.

N

Accessible parking

Key to grounds and monuments, above

1 Capitol
2 Capitol Extension
3 Hood's Brigade
4 Bicentennial Fountain
5 Heroes of the Alamo
6 Confederate Soldiers
7 Volunteer Firemen
8 Terry's Texas Rangers

9 Statue of Liberty replica
10 Texas Cowboy
11 The Hiker
12 Veterans of 36th Infantry
13 Texas Bicentennial Star
14 Ten Commandments
15 Pearl Harbor
16 Soldiers of World War I

17 Disabled American Veterans of Texas

Key to floorplans, at left

House offices

Senate offices

Governor's offices

Secretary of State's offices

Legislative library

Legislative Council

i Information and tours

t Telephones

e Elevators

w Women's restroom

m Men's restroom

+ First aid station

★ Security

Areas of interest

A House Gallery

B Senate Gallery

C House Chamber

D Governor's reception room

E Senate Chamber

F Rotunda floor (with seals of five nations of which Texas has been a part)

G Statues of Sam Houston and Stephen F. Austin

THE EXTENSION

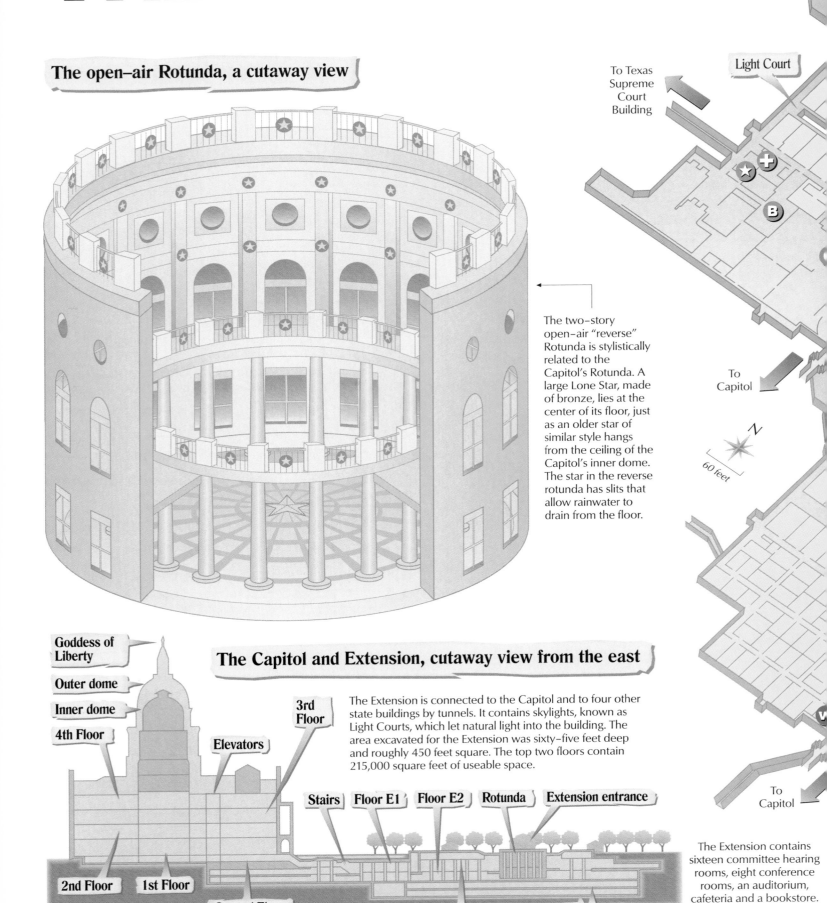

The open–air Rotunda, a cutaway view

To Texas Supreme Court Building

Light Court

To Capitol

60 feet

The two–story open–air "reverse" Rotunda is stylistically related to the Capitol's Rotunda. A large Lone Star, made of bronze, lies at the center of its floor, just as an older star of similar style hangs from the ceiling of the Capitol's inner dome. The star in the reverse rotunda has slits that allow rainwater to drain from the floor.

The Capitol and Extension, cutaway view from the east

Goddess of Liberty

Outer dome

Inner dome

4th Floor

Elevators

3rd Floor

The Extension is connected to the Capitol and to four other state buildings by tunnels. It contains skylights, known as Light Courts, which let natural light into the building. The area excavated for the Extension was sixty–five feet deep and roughly 450 feet square. The top two floors contain 215,000 square feet of useable space.

Stairs   Floor E1   Floor E2   Rotunda   Extension entrance

2nd Floor   1st Floor

Ground Floor

Central Light Court   Parking (legislative, not public)

100 feet

To Capitol

The Extension contains sixteen committee hearing rooms, eight conference rooms, an auditorium, cafeteria and a bookstore.

INDEX